LETTING GOD
BE JUDGE

LETTING GOD BE JUDGE

Recognizing the Impact of Ungodly Judgments and Dealing with them

Thomas J. Sappington

Sovereign World

Sovereign World Ltd
PO Box 784
Ellel
Lancaster LA1 9DA
England

Unless otherwise stated, all Scripture quotations are taken from the New
International Version. Copyright © 1973, 1978, 1984 by International Bible
Society.
Quotations marked NKJV are taken from the New King James Version,
copyright © 1983, 1992 by Thomas Nelson, Inc.

ISBN 978-1-85240-458-1

The publishers aim to produce books which will help to extend and build up
the Kingdom of God. We do not necessarily agree with every view expressed
by the authors, or with every interpretation of Scripture expressed. We expect
readers to make their own judgement in the light of their understanding of
God's Word and in an attitude of Christian love and fellowship.

Typeset by CRB Associates, Reepham, Norfolk

CONTENTS

Acknowledgments

In 1997 I began teaching on the topic of healing and spiritual conflict, which led ultimately to the founding of a ministry called Ambassadors of Renewal that has trained over a thousand pastors and lay leaders. This book grows out of some of the basic teachings that we offer in our level one training.

I would like to thank Peter Horrobin, Founder and Director of Ellel Ministries, both for his significant role in launching my wife and me in the ministries of healing and deliverance, but also for his role in recommending this manuscript to Sovereign World Publishers. Thanks as well to my father-in-law, Roger Tompkins, and my friend, Dave Carlson, for reading earlier drafts of the manuscript and making helpful suggestions. Finally, I would like to express my appreciation to the Ambassadors of Renewal team here in Central Java, Indonesia. Hopefully they have learned as much from me as I have from them.

Thanks are due as well to Mr Paul Stanier of Sovereign World for his advice and encouragement during the process of publication.

This book would never have been written had it not been for the faithful love, support, and advice of my wife, Katy. Our three children, Chris, Joel and Amanda, have also played a key role in my growth and understanding, and to them this book is dedicated. Through the joy I have experienced in my relationship with them, I have learned much about our heavenly Father's heart of love for His children.

INTRODUCTION

Several years ago I was counseling with a young couple who held a leadership position in a strategic church-planting ministry. As we talked together, I had a positive impression of them both personally and as leaders in their ministry. The wife was a tiny young woman with a sweet smile and a delightful sense of humor, while the husband radiated a gentle maturity and spirituality. There was one thing, however, that was troubling to both of them and, as we talked, became a source of concern to me as well.

Both of them reported that at times the wife would become very aggressive, seemingly doing all she could to provoke her husband and to create conflict between them. At those times this sweet young woman would insult him, taunt him, and mock him in the most degrading ways. As you might expect, this left the husband confused, angry and wounded, and usually resulted in a major conflict. The interesting thing, however, was that the wife herself was also confused by her own behavior. She had no idea why she was acting in a way that was so foreign to her.

As I talked to them and tried to be open to the Spirit's leading, I asked the wife a fairly obvious question, "Why do you think you do this?" She looked thoughtful yet confused for a moment, then she said, "Maybe I just want him to divorce me!" Wow, was I astounded by her response! Then I asked, "Why do you want him to divorce you?" After thinking for a second or two, she blurted out, "I guess I just want him to get on with it!"

At that moment the Spirit reminded me of her background and everything became clear. Her father was an abusive man who eventually abandoned the family. During the time he was a part of her life, he demonstrated a consistent pattern of unfaithfulness. It could almost be said that he never made a promise that he hadn't broken.

This sinful pattern of living had a major impact on his daughter. Besides allowing a tremendous load of bitterness to accumulate in her heart, at some point in her life this young woman had made a judgment against her father. This judgment expressed itself in the making of an inner vow. "I'll never marry a man who is abusive and unfaithful like him!" she vowed in her heart. In some cases women who have made this kind of judgment (and vow) against their father end up marrying someone just like him, but thankfully the Lord provided a gentle, godly, and trustworthy young man to be her husband. It looked as if she would live happily ever after.

Yet the judgment and the vow she made were still at work in her heart. In fact, the judgment was much bigger than she imagined. It included not only her father, but also all men, simply because they were the same gender as her father. She had the expectation that men in general were going to be like her father, and a number of men that she knew fitted the profile quite well. Though her husband's character was quite different, in her heart she was convinced that it was only a matter of time until he broke his marriage vows, leaving her wounded and disgraced. This deep conviction, as well as the fear that accompanied it, drove her to provoke him in an attempt to hasten the inevitable.

Thankfully the story has a happy ending. God gave me the wisdom to understand the basis for their problem, and the wife recognized immediately the truth of the diagnosis. She walked through the process of forgiving her father. Then she renounced both the judgment and the vow, repented of them, and broke the power of these things in her life. I checked on their progress some months later and was told that the couple was doing very well.

Unfortunately, not every story ends so happily. Over my years of experience in ministry as a pastor, a missionary, a seminary professor and a counselor, I have met many people who are disappointed with their spiritual growth. They really desire to know the Lord more intimately, to become like Jesus Christ, and to bless others in Christian service, but they are deeply frustrated. For them progress is painstakingly slow, and they often fall back into the same sinful, unhealthy patterns of thinking, of acting, and of relating to others. They don't understand why they struggle with flashes of uncontrolled anger and irrational thoughts, or why they have so much trouble in their relationships with their husbands or wives, their friends, or their co-workers. These believers are often deeply committed to Christ. They are faithful in prayer, read their Bibles daily, and wouldn't dream of missing public worship at their church, yet they find little joy in these Christian disciplines. Some of them struggle alone, while others pour out their hearts to their pastor or a Christian counselor. Although they recognize their need and are ready to seek help, they are unable to find someone who understands their struggle and can help them break free to true freedom and victory in Christ.

Years ago, in spite of my years of seminary training and several courses in psychology and counseling, I had few answers for believers who were in the midst of this battle. I knew I wanted to avoid spiritual-sounding yet superficial solutions, but in positive terms I really had very little to offer these brothers and sisters in Christ. Over the last ten years, however, I've learned to bring them to God in prayer and to allow Him apply His healing touch to their deepest wounds. He is the Great Physician and the Wonderful Counselor. Still, they cannot be merely passive recipients of His healing, for the Lord requires each of us to take certain steps toward healing and wholeness.

One critical step in the process of moving toward freedom and maturity in Christ is repenting of the ungodly judgments we have made against God, ourselves, and others, and breaking their power in our lives. Surprisingly, however, in spite of the fact that an astounding number of Christian books are published each year, it is rare to find a book or even an article that mentions the subject, much less one that is devoted to it.[1] As a result, pastors and counselors are often ill-equipped to deal with the judgments their counselees have made in the past and continue to make on a regular basis in the present. The struggle continues for many believers, and rarely do they receive the guidance they need even to understand the impact of ungodly judgments on their lives and their relationships, much less to repent of them and to destroy their power once and for all. This continuing struggle on the part of individual believers inevitably weakens local churches, and ultimately the whole body of Christ. Since churches can only be healthy and strong when their individual members are healthy and growing in Christ, the Bible's teaching on ungodly judgments is desperately needed for the health and growth of the Church of Jesus Christ.

The current lack of biblical teaching on this subject is complicated by the world's perception of "judgmentalism." For many people today, anytime a person believes or states that something is absolutely right or absolutely wrong, they are "judging" those who believe or behave differently. For such people, truth is relative, so that what is right for one person may not be right for another. In their eyes I am "judgmental" anytime I state that the actions of another person are wrong in an absolute sense. For example, if I state that the practice of homosexuality is contrary to God's design for humanity, then according to many people – including some Christians – I have already judged all practicing homosexuals. This point of view is far from the teaching of Scripture, which sets forth clear standards of right and wrong, yet at the same time prohibits strongly the sin of judging others. Certainly, then, one can believe in absolute truth and take a stand on a particular issue, but do so in a way that does not "judge" others in a negative sense.

As disciples of Christ, we must follow His teaching and example in this area. To return to the example of homosexuality, it is possible to affirm that the practice of homosexuality is contrary to God's design and will for humanity, but to do so in a manner that is not judgmental in a biblical sense, i.e. that maintains the worth and dignity of the homosexual. This is a lesson Christians desperately need to learn in this day and age.

On the one hand, some believers have abandoned biblical absolutes and have allowed the world to determine what is true and what is false as well as what is right and what is wrong.[2] I recently received an e-mail from a friend that illustrates this problem. He is involved in a ministry to help sexually broken people, including homosexuals, find healing and victory in a living, vital relationship with Christ. Just before a recent training event, he was visited by three men who objected strongly to his involvement with this seminar. In fact, they attacked him and his ministry vehemently, arguing that he should support people in their homosexuality rather than leading them to find healing and repentance. Given the current intellectual climate regarding homosexuality, this experience might not have been too surprising except for the fact that these three men were pastors! Instead of teaching their congregations to submit themselves to the clear teachings of Scripture, they were allowing the world to dictate their beliefs and their lifestyle. This would be grievous enough if it was an isolated incident, but the fact is that many in the Church today have abandoned biblical teachings and ethics in favor of more "enlightened" perspectives. In their attempt to avoid being "judgmental," they have completely set aside Jesus' teaching on the subject.

On the other hand, Christians must express their commitment to biblical teachings and ethics in a way that also reflects the love and grace of the Lord Jesus. Too often we speak the truth, but do so in such a judgmental manner that we forfeit any positive influence we might have had on the lives of others, especially those who have yet to know Christ as Lord and Savior. For example, I have often been appalled to see the response of some Christians to the "gay-rights movement." My problem is usually not with what they had to say, but rather with how they said it. Instead of responding in a spirit that reflects the heart of our Lord Jesus, that honors the sinner as one created in the image of God and therefore worthy of love, understanding, and ministry, Christians often present their views in the same strident and judgmental manner as the worldly activists to whom they are responding. As a result, in some cases the bitter and sometimes violent reactions they encounter are understandable. It is not enough merely to proclaim the truth; we must also do so *in love*, praying earnestly that God will lead the sinner to repentance and the knowledge of Himself, where he or she will find true healing and restoration.

The Church today needs a deeper understanding of the biblical teachings on ungodly judgments so that we can learn to speak God's truth in love. We must know when we are falling into the judgments that Jesus so clearly prohibits, and when we are simply standing for God's truth in a manner that brings glory and honor to Him. Only then can the Church present a strong testimony and lead many people into a saving knowledge of Jesus Christ. The fact is that nothing turns off non-Christians like a judgmental spirit. For that reason, we need a practical understanding of the biblical teaching on ungodly judgments so that the Church of Jesus Christ can effectively declare the gospel of grace that "teaches us to say 'No' to ungodliness and worldly passions, and to live self-controlled, upright and godly lives in this present age" (Titus 2:12).

In this study on ungodly judgments I am building on the foundation laid by John and Paula Sandford in their books *Restoring the Christian Family* and *The Transformation of the Inner Man*.[3] I learned much from their writings, especially in the early days of my ministry in the areas of inner healing and deliverance. I am, however, attempting to build something new on the foundation they have laid, so the reader will notice some differences between my approach and theirs.

I often say that I have seen more fruit in my ministry during the past ten years than in all the previous years put together. Much of this increased fruitfulness is due to the fact that I have learned to follow the Lord's leading in my counseling ministry and have utilized basic principles of inner healing and deliverance. Dealing with ungodly judgments is one of these principles, and it has been a blessing to God's people wherever I have shared it. My prayer is that this teaching will be a blessing to Christians all over the world and will lead countless believers to experience true freedom and victory in Jesus Christ. May the God of Grace, who loves us and accepts us completely in Christ, receive all glory and honor. Amen.

Notes

1. For this reason, I was delighted to see the article by Cindy Jacobs on this subject which appeared in two recently published collection of essays: "Releasing Bitter Root Judgments," in *Ministering Freedom to the Emotionally Wounded*, ed. Doris M. Wagner (Colorado Springs: Wagner Publications, 2003), 24–36, and, in a slightly revised form, in *How to Minister Freedom*, ed. Doris M. Wagner (Ventura, CA: Regal Books, 2005), 102–111, though I differ in some ways with her approach to the subject. Cf. the article by Karl D. Lehman and Charlotte E.T. Lehman, "Judgments and Bitterness as Clutter that Hinders Prayer for Emotional Healing," 19 June 2002 <http://www.kclehman.com> (which discusses

judgments and bitterness in relation to Theophostic ministry), as well as chapter 2, "Judge Not, that You Be Not Judged: Should We Stop Making Judgments?" in Erwin W. Lutzer, *Who are You to Judge?* (Chicago: Moody Publishers, 2002), 37–55, which contains sound biblical teaching on the subject in a limited format. Dallas Willard, *The Divine Conspiracy* (London: Fount Paperbacks, 1998), 237–254, also offers some insightful comments related to judging and condemning others.

2. This is the main burden of Lutzer in *Who are You to Judge?*; cf. Patrick Ramsey, "Judging According to the Bible," *Journal of Biblical Counseling* 21 (2002), 62–69.

3. John and Paula Sandford, *Restoring the Christian Family* (Tulsa, OK: Victory House, 1979), 196–211, and *The Transformation of the Inner Man* (Tulsa, OK: Victory House, 1982), 237–266. Their teachings on Bitter Root Judgments have also been prominent in their seminars, conferences, and their training events at Elijah House.

Chapter 1

UNGODLY JUDGMENTS
IN THE NEW TESTAMENT

I live my life in an uneasy tension. On the one hand, I am committed to biblical truth, which has led me into both personal and academic study of the Scriptures. I open the Word each morning in my personal devotions, and I have led many Bible studies. I have also preached hundreds of sermons and taught countless seminary classes over the years. During these years of study and ministry, my conviction that the Bible is truly the Word of God has not waned in the slightest. In fact, my level of confidence in the truth, authority, and power of God's Word is higher now than it has been at any point in my life. More than ever I love to dig into the Scriptures, to learn more about God and His will for my life, and to share what I learn with others.

On the other hand, I have a pastoral heart that longs to see others grow in their relationship with Christ. For this reason, it is not easy for me to admit that simply proclaiming God's Word has not produced the results I had hoped for in the lives of some of the believers to whom I have ministered. This was especially true during the earlier years of my ministry. During the last decade, however, I have learned to bring people to the Lord in prayer for healing and deliverance, and I have witnessed a dramatic increase in effectiveness and fruitfulness both in my own ministry and in the ministries of those I have trained. Make no mistake, the Word of God still plays a critical role in my life and ministry. Nothing has changed there. Now, however, the teaching of the Word is accompanied by powerful works of the Spirit as we wait on the Lord in prayer and allow God's Spirit to deepen our understanding of His truth and His love for us. I've also witnessed the power and authority of God's Word and God's Spirit working together to set hundreds of people free from the influence of demonic powers. It has been truly amazing to see what God has done, and how He has blown apart my narrow understanding of His work during the present age.

As a result of these experiences, I find myself in an uneasy alliance with others who are involved in the ministries of inner healing and deliverance. In many ways we talk the same language and share many of the same experiences, but I find that this identification brings with it a certain tension. In my experience, these ministries frequently attract people with a strong mystical orientation. Though such people are often used by God in powerful ways, the result of this tendency is, unfortunately, that a solid, biblical foundation is lacking in many of the teachings that are delivered in seminars or published in books on these subjects. In many cases fundamental ministry concepts and paradigms are created more on the basis of someone's experience than as a development of clear, biblical teachings and doctrines. Many writers in these fields then attempt to provide biblical support for their paradigms in the form of a list of proof-texts, many of which actually bear little relationship to the teachings in question. Needless to say, this lack of solid biblical and theological support undermines the confidence of many believers in these ministries and attracts needless criticism. In the end, many believers and many churches are hesitant to embrace the ministries of inner healing and deliverance, and so miss out on the tremendous blessings that they can bring.

In building a home, it is critical to lay a solid foundation. Otherwise, the entire structure could eventually collapse. In the same way, in our study of ungodly judgments, it is important to begin by considering carefully the biblical data on the subject. Only then can we be confident that the results of our study are in line with the teaching of God's Word. My goal, of course, is that the teaching contained in the following chapters will maintain biblical balance and become a blessing to the Church of Jesus Christ.

What is an ungodly judgment?

What exactly do we mean when we speak of "judging others" or "making a judgment against them"? At the most basic level, an ungodly judgment is a negative attitude, mindset, and set of expectations toward another, which can be directed toward God, ourselves, or others. It is often based on a deep-level deception regarding the other person or persons, about ourselves, or about our situation. Judgments often contain elements of truth, but they typically lack balance, tend to be fixed and unchangeable as well as harsh and uncompassionate, and often lead us to expect the worst of others.[1] Ungodly judgments can take various forms, from a mildly critical spirit to a deeply rooted attitude and expectation that controls much of a person's life. The nature of judgments will be examined more deeply in chapter 2, but at this point it is sufficient to note that we judge someone when we set our emotions, thoughts, and expectations against them. It is important to emphasize that we ourselves are the ones who "make a judgment." It is not something that suddenly befalls us or appears on its own. Rather, we ourselves make a choice to judge another person, even if we are unaware of what we are doing at the time.[2]

The importance of the command not to judge

Though I have studied the New Testament for many years, only recently did I make an in-depth study of the commands not to judge other people, especially fellow believers. What I discovered is that we are warned clearly and repeatedly of this danger. Evidently the Lord knows our tendencies better than we do ourselves. Four passages are prominent:

- Matthew 7:1–5 (cf. Luke 6:37–42, which is similar in a number of respects): "Do not judge, or you too will be judged" (v. 1). Jesus' command is reinforced with the illustration of the speck in our brother's eye and the plank in our own.
- Romans 14:9–13: "You, then, why do you judge your brother? Or why do you look down on your brother?" (v. 10). The point of this passage is that we should focus on repairing our own sins and shortcomings, for we are all accountable to God.
- James 2:1–4: "Have you not discriminated among yourselves and become judges with evil thoughts?" (v. 4). The issue at hand in this passage is discrimination against poorer brothers and sisters in Christ and in favor of the rich.
- James 4:11–12: "Anyone who speaks against his brother or judges him speaks against the law and judges it" (v. 11). The context reminds us that there is "only one Lawgiver and Judge."

A number of supporting verses also bring out the dangers of judging others:

- Romans 2:1: "You, therefore, have no excuse, you who pass judgment on someone else, for at whatever point you judge the other, you are condemning yourself, because you who pass judgment do the same things."
- 1 Corinthians 4:5: Therefore judge nothing before the appointed time; wait till the Lord comes. He will bring to light what is hidden in darkness and will expose the

motives of men's hearts. At that time each will receive his praise from God.

- 1 Corinthians 10:29–30: For why should my freedom be judged by another's conscience? If I take part in the meal with thankfulness, why am I denounced because of something I thank God for?

In addition to the number of passages that make reference to the sin of judging others, we should note the solemn nature of the warnings. When we judge others, we bring judgment on ourselves (Matthew 7:1–5), we have "evil thoughts" (James 2:1–4), we judge God's law (James 4:11–12), and we "condemn ourselves" (Romans 2:1). Certainly judging others is not a trivial matter from God's perspective.

Why are judgments off-limits for believers?

Given the fact that we rarely read a book or hear a sermon on the topic of ungodly judgments, the number of New Testament passages on the subject, as well as the tenor of those passages, is surprising. Why does the New Testament teach us clearly and repeatedly not to judge others? If we study these passages in relation to the whole of the New Testament, the answer is obvious. The simple fact is that judging others is incompatible with three foundational principles in Jesus' teaching and the teaching of His disciples. This incompatibility is the basis for the specific prohibitions in Scripture and helps us understand why judging others is inappropriate for those who call themselves followers of Christ.

Judging others is incompatible with the gracious way God treats us in Christ

When we read the parable of the unmerciful servant in Matthew 18:21–35, it is interesting to note the reaction of both "the other servants" and "the master" to the servant's harsh treatment of "one of his fellow servants who owed him a hundred denarii" (v. 28). In verse 31 we read,

> "When the other servants saw what had happened, they were greatly distressed and went and told their master everything that had happened."

The reaction of the master in verses 32–34 is even more notable:

> "Then the master called the servant in. 'You wicked servant,' he said, 'I cancelled all that debt of yours because you begged me to. Shouldn't you have had mercy on your fellow servant just as I had on you?' In anger his master turned him over to the jailers to be tortured, until he should pay back all he owed."

Why are the servants "greatly distressed" and why is the master moved to respond "in anger"? The parties involved respond in this way because the servant's treatment of his fellow servant is not only inappropriate, it is sinful. The master addresses him as "You wicked servant" (v. 32). Having received grace from the master, who forgave the man's debt of astronomical proportions, he now does the unthinkable. He approaches his fellow servant harshly ("He grabbed him and began to choke him," v. 28). He demands immediate payment of his fellow servant's proportionately insignificant debt. He refuses the man's request for extra time and ignores his promise to repay what he owed. And, finally, he has him thrown into prison "until he could pay the debt" (v. 30), that is, indefinitely.

Something is very wrong here, and everyone recognizes it. The fellow servants are "greatly distressed," the master responds "in anger," and the parable plainly states that God's point of view is not all that different,

> This is how my heavenly Father will treat each of you unless
> you forgive your brother from your heart.

(v. 35)

The simple fact is that people who receive grace should be ready and willing to extend it to others. God's grace flows into our lives from the moment we accept Christ as our Lord and Savior. It should not stop there, however. Rather, God's grace should then flow out from us to other people as we accept them, bear with them, forgive them, and refuse to judge them. An unwillingness to do this demonstrates a wickedness of heart that is inconsistent with God's gracious work in a believer's life. This is not to say that as believers we will always avoid the trap of making ungodly judgments against others. None of us is perfect. However, as those who have received grace and forgiveness from our heavenly Father, we should be willing to open our hearts and to release any judgments we might have made against them. Since God in His abundant grace has chosen not to judge us in Christ, we must resist the temptation to sit in judgment on others for their sins and shortcomings.

Judging others is incompatible with a life of humility

The fact is that truly humble people rarely make ungodly judgments because they maintain a balanced view of themselves and others. They understand and apply Paul's words in Romans 12:3,

> Do not think of yourself more highly than you ought, but
> rather think of yourself with sober judgment...

They know that they themselves have strengths and weaknesses, and that they struggle with sin – both attitudinal and behavioral – in certain areas of their lives. They know that they are far from perfect, and they recognize their need to receive ministry as well as to minister to others. They are able to rejoice in the strengths and successes of others without feeling threatened because they know that God uses a variety of gifts and personalities to strengthen the body of Christ and to bring glory to Himself.

Because humble people have a balanced view of their own lives and ministries, they tend to be more patient with others and accepting of them in spite of their sins and shortcomings. This does not mean that they do not challenge others to overcome these negative characteristics, but they do so patiently and in love, knowing that sanctification is a process that takes some time. Humble people do not quickly write others off or slap a negative label on them because of their sin. They acknowledge the areas of growth and maturity where they are evident and pray in faith that these qualities will extend to every area of their lives.

In addition, humble people recognize the potential others have to serve God and to glorify His name, in spite of their limitations and shortcomings. They acknowledge the spiritual gifts the Lord has given to other believers, even if those gifts are in the early stages of development, and recognize that the Lord often calls imperfect people to undertake significant ministries for His glory.

Such people choose to follow Paul's admonition in Philippians 2:3,

> Do nothing out of selfish ambition or vain conceit, but in humility consider others better than yourselves.

Instead of judging the other person for their sin or spiritual immaturity, they focus on building up the person and helping them become all they can be in Christ. They recognize that, ultimately, the other person's life and ministry may be more significant than their own, and they rejoice in the potential achievements of their brothers and sisters in Christ.

Back in 1980, when I entered Trinity Evangelical Divinity School for my seminary training, I had the privilege of taking my first theology class from the late Dr Kenneth Kantzer. After doing my undergraduate work at a state university, I was excited to have the opportunity to study God's Word, and Dr Kantzer was an outstanding teacher. However, not all the students received his teaching with enthusiasm. Several students, who had studied Bible and theology at the bachelor's level before coming to Trinity, took exception to some of his teachings. I remember that they argued with him vigorously and emotionally, in a way that at times bordered on disrespect. What struck me, however, was that this mature man of God always answered them gently, patiently, and with obvious humility. He did not judge them in his heart, but recognized that God was still at work in their lives. While I must admit that I have forgotten many of the details of what he taught in that course, I still remember his example of humility as a Christian man and a Christian teacher. In fact, some students here in Indonesia have commented that they appreciate the way I answer students' questions and objections gently and patiently, a tendency that I acquired by emulating Dr Kantzer's interactions with students.

When we make ungodly judgments against others, we usually do so out of our own pride or, in some cases, our own insecurities. In either case, we are straying far from God's purpose for us. In addition, when we judge others we often focus so much on our brother's or sister's sin and short-comings that we forget about our own. As a result our perspective is skewed, and we do not express the attitude of humility that God desires for each of us.

Judging others is incompatible with the fact that only God has the right to judge

Imagine how you would feel if a complete stranger walked into your home, kicked off his shoes, opened your refrigerator, helped himself to a big glass of milk and a sandwich, and plopped down in front of your television set with his feet up on your coffee table. You would be shocked and perhaps fearful, of course, but you would also be filled with a sense of outrage. This person has no right to be in your home, but he is acting as if he is completely within his rights to enter your home, eat your food, and watch your television, all without asking permission.

I am certain God feels this same sense of outrage when we judge our brothers and sisters in Christ. The Bible's teaching on this matter is absolutely clear. Only God has the right to judge:

> There is only one Lawgiver and Judge, the one who is able to save and to destroy. But you – who are you to judge your neighbor?
>
> (James 4:12)

How then can we act as if we have the right to judge our neighbor when only God Himself has this right? We are no different than that stranger who makes himself at home in our house. We are living outside of our rights.

This clear and unambiguous teaching of Scripture contradicts the deep-rooted deception that leads many believers to maintain their judgments against others. As one pastor's wife said, "Why shouldn't I hate my dad? And why shouldn't I judge him? Look at what he did to me!" When she said that, I could see her point. Her dad had rejected her, setting her up for a life of abuse and further rejection as she was passed around from one relative to another. As a result, she felt that she had a right to hate him and to judge him. And while I could understand her feelings, I knew that Scripture teaches otherwise. Just as God gave up His true right to judge us for our sins and to condemn us to eternal punishment, so she needed to lay down her "right" to judge her father. In her case, as in the lives of many other people to whom we have ministered, this step of obedience opened the door for her to experience true healing and freedom from the wounds of her past. Interestingly enough, her husband came to me after she had received ministry several times from our team and said, "I'd like whatever it was that my wife received." Apparently the transformation in her had not gone unnoticed!

If we are open at all to the teaching of Scripture, we must acknowledge that judging others contradicts some of the most fundamental teachings of the New Testament. It is incompatible with grace, it is incompatible with humility, and it is incompatible with the fact that only God has the right to judge. Clearly it is sin. Many believers are vaguely aware of the New Testament teachings on this topic, but they are unsure when they are judging others. That is why we need some detailed guidelines to help us discern when we are making judgments against others and falling into sinful thoughts and attitudes.

Notes

1. In my experience judgments rarely lack some objective basis, which is why they are so common and so dangerous.

2. This principle is consistent with the fact that we are commanded to avoid the temptation to judge others (see the verses cited in the next section of this chapter). If God commands us to do something (or to avoid something), the implication is that we are responsible to obey His commands *in humble dependence on the power of the Holy Spirit.*

Chapter 2

Godly Discernment versus Ungodly Judgments

One area of confusion for many believers is the difference between godly discernment and ungodly judgments.[1] Clearly as believers we must use Spirit-led discernment in our relationships with others. Jesus makes this clear in the immediate context of Matthew 7:1–5, one of the primary New Testament passages about judging others. In verse 6 we are instructed,

> "Do not give dogs what is sacred; do not throw your pearls to pigs. If you do, they may trample them under their feet, and then turn and tear you to pieces."

Following Jesus' instruction clearly involves first determining who is a "dog" and who is a "pig," i.e. who is "persistently vicious, irresponsible, and unappreciative."[2] We should not attempt to share our most precious spiritual truths with such people as our "pearls" will only serve to enrage them.

In the same context Jesus also commands us to watch out for "false prophets" who come in sheep's clothing (Matthew 7:15), but who bear bad fruit and are ultimately condemned as "evildoers" (Matthew 7:23). In both cases we are instructed to

use our God-given discernment in our relationships with
others, and the context demonstrates that this in no way
contradicts Jesus' command not to judge our brothers and
sisters in Christ. Discerning and judging are clearly two
different things.

Not only Jesus' teaching but our general experience of the
Christian life also demonstrates the need for godly discernment. Several examples come to mind. When we elect (or
appoint) church leaders such as elders and deacons, the
Apostle Paul assumes that we will choose those whose lives
fit the criteria laid out in 1 Timothy (3:1–13) and Titus (1:6–9).
This requires the use of godly discernment. Also, if we are
involved in the ministry of discipleship, as was Timothy, we are
instructed to focus our attention on "reliable men who will also
be qualified to teach others" (2 Timothy 2:2). Once again, you
can't do this without godly discernment.

The challenge for us as believers is to determine when
we're using proper discernment in our relationships with
others, and when we're sitting in judgment on them. This is
no easy task, and many believers are confused about the two
approaches. If we look carefully at Scripture, however, there
are a number of clues that can help us understand the
difference. From these clues I have developed a number of
criteria that can help us to evaluate our own responses to
others. Of course, not all of these criteria will be applicable in
every case. However, by looking at our attitudes toward others
from a variety of perspectives, we can gain clarity that would
be impossible if we were assessing our attitudes from only one
direction.

I have formulated these criteria by using eight questions.
By answering these questions honestly and openly, we give
the Spirit an opportunity to show us whether we've made
judgments against others, or are using godly discernment in
our relationships with them.

Question 1: Would we be comfortable if they viewed and evaluated us in the same way we are evaluating them?

This is a specific application of the golden rule,

> "So in everything, do to others what you would have them do to you, for this sums up the Law and the Prophets."
> (Matthew 7:12; cf. Luke 6:31; Romans 13:8–10)

This principle requires us to imagine ourselves in their position, i.e. as the one who is being evaluated. Would we feel comfortable if they were evaluating us in the same way in which we are evaluating them? If so, then we are probably using godly discernment rather than sitting in judgment on them. The manner and the spirit in which we are evaluating them are the critical factors. Are we evaluating them in a sincere, careful, gentle, and loving manner, i.e. a manner in which we ourselves would like to be evaluated? If so, then we are probably using godly discernment in our relationship to them.

If, on the other hand, we become uncomfortable when we imagine ourselves trading places with them, then we may very well be sitting in judgment on them. Why is that? The reality is that no one likes to be judged. In fact, Jesus' teaching in the Sermon on the Mount is based on this assumption, "Do not judge, or you too will be judged" (Matthew 7:1). He assumes that we will wish to avoid being judged, and on that basis He urges us not to judge others. Judgments tend to involve a harshness of spirit, an insensitivity to the person's background and current situation, a lack of faith and charity, and a tendency to define things in terms of black and white. All these things can make us uncomfortable, frustrated, hurt, and even angry when we are on the receiving end of a judgment.

I remember several years ago this question was very helpful in my life. As a missionary, I must work with all kinds of people, both nationals and foreigners. At one point I became very negative in my thoughts and feelings toward another missionary who had been on the field for many years. The fact is I just did not like his way of dealing with other people, and indeed his weaknesses in this area were evident to many people. Still, my attitude toward him was not right.

One day as I was reading the Bible and praying, I sensed the Holy Spirit saying, "How would you feel if he judged you as harshly as you have judged him?" As I thought about it I realized that I had judged him in my heart. Instead of seeing him as a faithful servant of Christ who just happened to have certain weaknesses, all I could think of was what a jerk he was! I then realized how unfair I was being to him, and how I would not at all care to have someone else judge me in the same way I had judged him. I repented of my attitude and our relationship improved significantly, even though his weaknesses remained.

By trading places with the person we are evaluating, we can gain insight into our own attitude toward them. If we imagine ourselves in the other person's position, how would we feel if we were evaluated in the manner and spirit with which we are evaluating them? If we would feel uncomfortable being evaluated in this matter, then our reaction should serve as a strong warning to us. We may very well have crossed the line that separates godly discernment from ungodly judgments.

Question 2: Are we giving proper attention to their strengths as well as their weaknesses?

Every person has strengths and weaknesses, and many times our weaknesses are the flip side of our strengths. For example, one of the qualities that enables me to write books and articles is my ability to focus in and concentrate on the task at hand. That is a strength, but it can also be a weakness or a liability in certain situations. I don't multi-task well, and sometimes I am so absorbed in my research and writing that I miss an appointment or forget to pick up the kids. I am aware of this weakness, and I attempt to compensate for it by looking at my calendar daily and sticking big notes around the edges of my computer screen, but occasionally something will fall through the cracks in my system.

I am so thankful that my wife, Katy, does not judge me for this weakness (and this is only one of many!). She values my ability as a teacher and a writer, and she understands that my tendency sometimes to get lost in the world of ideas is just a part of the bigger picture of who I am. She helps me to keep track of things, but when something falls through the cracks in my system, she doesn't sit in judgment on me. Rather, she bears with me in love (Colossians 3:13; cf. Romans 15:1).[3]

Most of the time we are using godly discernment when we understand a person's weaknesses, but see them as only a part of who they are. We're also aware of their strengths, and recognize that God has gifted them in certain ways for His glory. When we fall into the trap of judging others, however, we are in a very dangerous place. Oblivious to our own sins and shortcomings, we become fixated on the faults of others.[4] In Jesus' words, we focus in (continuously) on the "speck in our brother's eye" (Matthew 7:3–5; cf. Luke 6:41). In fact, their "speck" is often all we see. At this point, we typically lose balance in our perspective on the other person. Our eyes are so filled with their sins and shortcomings that we can't see anything else, including their personal strengths and their giftedness in certain critical areas. We might even say that we begin to define them in terms of their shortcomings and their sin. When that happens, we can be fairly certain that we have judged them in our heart.

Question 3: Are we developing "spiritual far-sightedness"?

When our eyes become filled with the sins and shortcomings of others, we often lose balance not only in our assessment of them, but also in our assessment of ourselves. Like a person who is severely far-sighted, we can see clearly the sins and faults of others, but we are blind to our own transgressions and shortcomings. To use Jesus' words, the "speck in our brother's eye" seems so massive in its proportions and overwhelming in its significance that we are utterly oblivious to the "plank in our own eye" (Matthew 7:3–5; Luke 6:41–42). At that point we have fallen into the hypocrisy that Jesus so vigorously condemns (Matthew 7:5; Luke 6:42; cf. especially Matthew 23).

How easy it is for us as believers to fall into this trap! I don't know how many times the Holy Spirit has stopped me over the years as I was about to make a judgment against someone else because of a sin or shortcoming, and pointed out to me the fact that I myself was not without fault in that same area or in some other important area of my life. Hypocrisy of this nature is especially common when we are guilty of sins of the heart such as a critical spirit, self-centeredness, self-righteousness, or a tendency toward legalism.[5] We can find ourselves falling into the trap described in Romans 2:1:

> You, therefore, have no excuse, you who pass judgment on someone else, for at whatever point you judge the other, you are condemning yourself, because you who pass judgment do the same things.

This kind of hypocrisy is exactly what we see in the parable of the Pharisee and the Tax Collector (Luke 18:9–14), which Jesus told for the benefit of those "who were confident of their own righteousness and looked down on everybody else" (v. 9). The Pharisee's judgment was very broad indeed: "God, I thank you that I am not like other men – robbers, evildoers, adulterers – or even like this tax collector." Clearly his focus was on external behavior. He knew that he had not committed gross sins – which were very common indeed among tax collectors – and that he was scrupulous in his adherence to the Jewish law. "I fast twice a week and give a tenth of all I get," he boasted in his heart at the very moment he was offering worship to the Holy One of Israel (v. 12).

The Pharisee seemed completely unaware of his own pride and self-righteousness, the ungodly comparisons he was drawing with others, and the fact that he was sitting in judgment on a large segment of humanity. His hypocrisy should serve as a warning to us, who can easily fall into this pattern!

In addition to the sinful attitudes and actions with which we currently struggle, we also need to realize our own vulnerability to other sins, including the sin committed by the person we are tempted to judge. When we read the Apostle Paul's exhortation to the Galatians, it is humbling to recognize our own weakness:

> Brothers, if someone is caught in a sin, you who are spiritual should restore him gently. But watch yourself, or you also may be tempted.
>
> (Galatians 6:1)

The simple fact is that none of us is immune to temptation, and all of us have our own sin and shortcomings. If this is the case, how can we presume to sit in judgment on our brothers and sisters in Christ?

Question 4: Are we hoping, believing, and praying that they can change for the better?

We can be relatively sure that we are using godly discernment in our relationships with others when we recognize their sins and shortcomings, but maintain an attitude of faith and holy optimism toward them, choosing to believe that they have the potential to grow and mature in the Lord Jesus Christ. We have judged them, however, when we write them off, slapping a negative label on them that will stay with them for the rest of their days. I believe this is what Jesus had in mind when He spoke of someone calling out contemptuously to his brother, "You fool!" (Matthew 5:22). Such judgments can become a stumbling block in the life of the person we have judged, as well as hindering the development of our relationship with them.

My sister-in-law has taught in the public school system in California for many years, and I have heard her speak a number of times about the power a negative label can have in the life of a child. Early in their career in the public schools, children can be tagged with a negative label such as "troubled," "slow," or "difficult to discipline." These labels can have a lasting effect on children as it is very difficult for them to escape from a judgment that was made at one point in time, then passed on from one teacher to another.

I believe a similar yet deeper principle is at work in the spiritual realm. Often we slap negative judgments on a person that make it difficult for them to grow in the Lord, when in reality we should pray for them and wait patiently for God's gracious work in their life. The reality is that all of us are in process as believers.

How thankful I am that my parents and other adults in my life did not sit in judgment on me during the difficult years of high school when I professed faith but did not walk the walk. I had such a temper that two different varsity tennis coaches threatened to kick me off the team due to my outbursts and temper tantrums on the court! How easy it would have been for significant adults in my life to judge me at that point! The fact is I had a lot of rough edges at that stage in my life, but God wasn't finished with me yet. Later, when an older believer took an interest in me and began teaching and discipling me on a personal basis, I started growing rapidly as a Christian. Ultimately, I was called to serve God as a pastor, and at this time I have been a missionary in Indonesia for about thirteen years. Thank God for the committed adults who stuck with me during those early years of my Christian life. May He give me the same grace to stick with other believers who are still struggling with particular weaknesses and sins.

How can we know if we are using godly discernment rather than judging someone in an ungodly way? We need to look at our attitude toward them. Have we slapped a negative label on another person that will be difficult for them to escape? Do we see certain negative characteristics as fixed and unchangeable in their lives? Or are we choosing to believe that God – for whom nothing is impossible – is still in the business of changing lives? Are we choosing to love them with the love of Christ Himself, the love that hopes all things and believes all things (1 Corinthians 13:7)?

Question 5: Are we evaluating their behavior rather than speculating about their hidden motives and intentions?

One thing that Scripture teaches clearly is that only God knows what is in a person's heart. For example, this assumption underlies the prayer of the early believers in Acts 1:24–25:

> Then they prayed, "Lord, you know everyone's heart. Show us which of these two you have chosen to take over this apostolic ministry, which Judas left to go where he belongs."

When the early believers met to decide who would take Judas' place among the twelve apostles, they knew that they were dependent on God to show them what was in the men's hearts. Of course, they themselves could speculate based on their observation of the men's behavior, but their conclusions regarding the men's motives and intentions could be wrong. This limitation is simply a part of being human.

When we read the Apostle Paul's writings, we find a direct

warning against speculating about the motives and intentions of others:

> Therefore judge nothing before the appointed time; wait till the Lord comes. He will bring to light what is hidden in darkness and will expose the motives of men's hearts. At that time each will receive his praise from God.
>
> (1 Corinthians 4:5)

If we study the context of this verse, it is clear that this warning grew out of Paul's personal experience with the church in Corinth. Though his conscience was clear (v. 4), some members of the congregation were judging him, probably based on unhealthy comparisons with Peter and Apollos (3:21–22; 4:6).

In my experience, this is one of the most hurtful experiences associated with leadership. When we are truly seeking God's will for the people under us, and someone judges us based on their negative speculations about our motives, it puts a leader in a difficult position. Since the judgment relates to the attitudes and desires of their heart and not external behavior that can be observed, there is no way to show the person that their judgment is in error. In such a case, the leader can only affirm his desire to serve, continue to do what he is doing, and trust that over time God will bring the truth to light. I am thankful that I have rarely experienced this kind of judgment, because it is both hurtful and discouraging to every leader.

The fact is that we do not really know what is in another person's thoughts, motives, or desires. It is amazing how often I myself am wrong when I seek to understand what is in a person's heart. What looks like pride is often really insecurity. What I interpret as hardness of heart is often really inner woundedness. Actually, my inability to discern the thoughts, motives, and desires of others shouldn't surprise me. The fact is I am sometimes confused about my own motives and desires! Many times they are mixed, and sometimes I find myself thinking one thing and feeling another. If I can't even understand what is in my own heart, how can I claim to know what is in another person's heart?

And yet jumping to conclusions without adequate confirmation is exactly what we tend to do when we judge others. We do not merely evaluate their behavior as we observe it, but we also attempt to go much deeper. We speculate about their desires and motives, which can lead to various negative labels such as "proud," "arrogant," or "egotistical." The fact is that such labels are often mistaken, and even when they contain an element of truth, they are rarely helpful in our relationships with others or our ministries to them.

During our time in Indonesia, one of the things we as a family have observed in the Indonesian culture is how quickly people are labeled "proud" in a negative sense. When a person moves to a new area, for example, they are responsible to take the initiative in establishing relationships with their neighbors. If, however, they rarely emerge from their home, don't attend the neighborhood meetings, and seldom spend time visiting with their neighbors, this leaves the community with a very negative impression. They are inevitably labeled "proud." In reality, however, there are quite a number of possible explanations for their behavior. They may be shy or afraid to meet new people. They may be depressed or overwhelmed with responsibilities. They may come from another area or culture where the expectations are different. These possibilities are rarely considered, however. Right or wrong they are judged to be "proud," and all interactions from then on are filtered through this judgment.

If we find ourselves speculating in a negative way about another person's motives or desires, we may very well be falling into sin ourselves. On the other hand, if we tend to evaluate only the behavior that we can observe, then we have probably not crossed the line from godly discernment to ungodly judgments.

Question 6: Do we regard them as brothers and sisters in Christ rather than looking down on them because of their sins and shortcomings?

The key scripture here is Romans 14:9–10:

> For this very reason, Christ died and returned to life so that he might be the Lord of both the dead and the living. You, then, why do you *judge your brother*? Or why do you *look down on your brother*? For we will all stand before God's judgment seat.
>
> (emphasis added)

It is important to note the parallelism in verse 10 between judging and looking down on a brother or sister in Christ. Clearly the two attitudes are closely related. When we focus our attention on the sins and shortcomings of others and are oblivious to the "plank" in our own life, we inevitably fall into ungodly comparisons. We see ourselves as "more mature," "more spiritual," or "more obedient to God," often based on our adherence to our own set of values and standards. As was the case in Romans 14, these standards are frequently extra-biblical. Yet we use them as the basis for viewing ourselves as superior and our brother or sister as inferior morally or spiritually. At that point we have crossed the line from using godly discernment to making ungodly judgments.

The key principle here is that we must evaluate our own point of view. If we regard another person as a brother or sister who is equal to us in the Lord Jesus Christ, then we probably have not judged them in our heart. If, however, we view them from a superior position spiritually or morally, then there is a good chance that we have crossed the line from godly discernment to ungodly judgments.

How easy it is to look down on our brothers and sisters in Christ! Many of us, without even realizing it, have developed our own, usually extra-scriptural, criteria for evaluating the spirituality of others. In Romans 14 this is certainly the case. Two issues were potentially divisive, namely (1) whether believers ate "everything," including meat that had been offered to idols or, just to be safe, ate vegetables only (14:2–4, 6), and (2) whether believers regarded one day as special or considered every day alike (14:5–6). Given Paul's emphasis in the broader context of Romans 14, it seems that these issues had the potential to be divisive. Believers were in danger of turning these matters into criteria for evaluating the spirituality of their brothers and sisters in Christ. In short, they were in danger of developing a judgmental spirit.

It is interesting to read Paul's threefold response to this danger. First, he reminds them that it is not their place to judge their brothers or sisters in Christ:

> The man who eats everything must not look down on him who does not, and the man who does not eat everything must not condemn the man who does, for God has accepted him. Why are you to judge someone else's servant? To his own master he stands or falls. And he will stand, for the Lord is able to make him stand.
>
> (vv. 3–4)

Second, he informs them that their personal decisions on these matters are not that important in the Lord's eyes, for He cares about the attitude of their heart.[6] Are they doing what they are doing because they sincerely desire to do what is pleasing to Him? The answer to this question is more important to the Lord than whether they eat meat or not:

> One man considers one day more sacred than another; another man considers every day alike. Each one should be fully convinced in his own mind. He who regards one day as special, does so to the Lord. He who eats meat, eats to the Lord, for he

gives thanks to God; and he who abstains, does so to the Lord and gives thanks to God.

(vv. 5–6)

Third, he reminds us to think of the impact of our own behavior on our brothers and sisters in Christ. This should be our greatest concern, not whether or not other Christians are conforming to our own standards of conduct:

> Therefore let us stop passing judgment on one another. Instead, make up your mind not to put any stumbling block or obstacle in your brother's way.

(v. 13)

Often the issues are different in today's world, but the principle is the same. We can judge other believers based on many things, including their dress or appearance, their denomination, whether they go to movies or not, whether they use our particular version of the Bible, or whether they worship God in the way that is most comfortable for us. Such things, which are usually not addressed directly in the Scriptures, can become our standard for determining whether other people are spiritual or not.

I myself have never been a part of a church or Christian group that has had a large set of extra-biblical beliefs or standards for living, but I have known a number of people who have been a part of these groups. I heard of one woman who actually asked a pastor repeatedly not to wear his wedding ring. She said she didn't believe Christians should wear jewelry, and that when she saw him standing in the pulpit wearing his simple gold wedding band this became a stumbling block to her!

Sometimes my relationships with believers from this type of background have been very warm even though we had different perspectives on many things, while in other cases I have felt judged because I didn't adhere to their beliefs and standards. What has become clear to me over the years, however, is that I myself have often been tempted to look down on these brothers and sisters, and to view myself as having a superior understanding of the Scriptures. If I succumb to that temptation, however, then I will have fallen into the trap of judging my brother instead of loving him and seeking to build him up in Christ.

The fact is that our supposed "knowledge" and "understanding" can lead to pride and a judgmental spirit, while love leads us to focus our attention on our brother's needs rather than our own. "Knowledge puffs up, but love builds up," Paul writes in 1 Corinthians 8:1. This is a key principle as we attempt to distinguish between godly discernment and ungodly judgments. Ultimately, God doesn't care so much about our knowledge in non-scriptural matters, but about the attitude of love and the desire to please Him that exists in our hearts.

Question 7: Are we discriminating against certain groups of people?

We can make judgments against certain groups of people, not only against individuals. This principle is stated clearly in James 2:1–4:

> My brothers, as believers in our glorious Lord Jesus Christ, don't show favoritism. Suppose a man comes into your meeting wearing a gold ring and fine clothes, and a poor man in shabby clothes also comes in. If you show special attention to the man wearing fine clothes and say, "Here's a good seat for you," but say to the poor man, "You stand there" or "Sit on the floor by my feet," have you not discriminated among yourselves and become judges with evil thoughts?

Obviously the believer who treats the rich man in one way and the poor man in another has divided the church into two groups, the rich and the poor, and is discriminating between them. He has "judged" the poor group as unworthy of the same love and respect that he freely demonstrates to the rich. James soundly condemns them both for their "judgment" and their actions.

Clearly discrimination between rich and poor can happen in the body of Christ. However, socioeconomic status is by no means the only basis on which judgments can be made. We can also make judgments based on other factors such as gender, race, or position.

The reality is that as Christians we often make judgments, not only against another person, but also more broadly against the group of people they represent. Such judgments typically form the basis for all types of racism and prejudice. And once they have taken root in our lives, they can be passed down to the next generation, consciously or unconsciously. These inherited judgments, then, both limit and color our relationships with certain classes of people, so that the judgments are reinforced by interactions that take place in a context loaded with suspicion and negative expectations. After a while, the judgment-system becomes self-perpetuating.

It is interesting how sometimes we can slip into judging certain groups of people without even realizing it. Since we moved to Indonesia in 1993, one of the challenges we have faced is driving on the two-lane roads that connect the major cities on the island of Java, which is home to 110 million people! When we use our car, we must share the road with every form of transportation, including pedicabs, horse carts, bicycles, motorcycles, cars, mini-buses, large buses, and trucks. Of course, the driving style of most of the people is very different from that in the West. It actually reminds me of a demolition sport!

One thing that has become clear to me is that the large buses are king of the road here in Indonesia. They often pass without even checking the distance to the oncoming traffic, and it is up to the other drivers on the road to get out of their way. In fact, our family has been literally run off the road quite a number of times by careless bus drivers.

Without realizing it, these experiences had an influence on my attitude toward bus drivers. One day my wife told me that I was driving too aggressively and that she was afraid to ride with me. Her comment really took me by surprise since she had ridden with me for many years without a problem. As I prayed about her comment, I realized that I was angry with the bus drivers for behaving so outrageously on the road, and I had judged them in my heart. I assumed the worse, not only of a particular driver, but of all bus drivers on the island of Java. Now that's a big judgment!

The outworking of my anger and judgment was that I wasn't going to let them push me around, which is insane given the fact that our van is tiny compared to the large buses that travel on the main roads around Java. Thanks to my wife's rebuke, however, I forgave the drivers who had run me off the road in the past and repented of the judgment that I had made against them as a group. Since that time my wife has been much more relaxed when she rides with me!

In the context of our personal counseling ministry, we often encounter believers whose lives are being influenced by judgments they have made in the past. It's amazing, for example, how a person's life and marriage can be influenced powerfully by judgments they have made against an abusive father or mother. Frequently such judgments are not only against the parent in question, but are also against all persons of the same gender as that parent. And, sometimes, people who have had traumatic experiences early in life judge virtually all of humanity. As a result, they tend to approach relationships of every kind with suspicion and negative expectations that limit and color subsequent interactions, thus reinforcing the original judgment and strengthening its grip on their lives.

As we examine our own hearts, we need to ask ourselves honestly whether we are discriminating against different people or groups of people. If we are, then that is often a good indication that we have crossed over the line that distinguishes godly discernment from ungodly judgments.

Question 8: Are we consciously choosing to leave judgment in God's hands?

The New Testament teaches that only God has the right to judge a person's life and actions. This principle is stated clearly in James 4:12:

> There is only one Lawgiver and Judge, the one who is able to save and destroy. But you – who are you to judge your neighbor?
> (cf. 1 Corinthians 4:5; Romans 14:9–12)

Many times in relationships with others we are hurt, offended, or sinned against, whether intentionally or unintentionally. When this happens, we are tempted to hold anger and bitterness in our hearts, to make judgments against the person, and to seek revenge. A good way to tell if we are using godly discernment in our relationships with others is to ask ourselves if we are consciously leaving judgment in God's hands, in spite of the injustice of our current situation. If we are, then there is a good chance that we are using godly discernment and have not fallen into the trap of making judgments against them.

Why does God reserve the right to judge men and women? In the end, I believe, it comes down to the fact that only He understands fully our individual situations, so that only He is qualified to sit as judge. I have frequently witnessed the limitations of human understanding in personal ministry sessions. One of the things that often happens in prayer for inner healing is that God reveals to us things about our situation that were previously unknown to us, which leads to a change in our feelings, our attitudes and our responses toward others. For example, when a wife is having trouble forgiving the unfaithfulness of her husband, the Lord sometimes reveals the deep rejection and woundedness he experienced as a child. This new understanding reduces her to tears, softens her heart toward her husband, and enables her to take the critical step of forgiving her husband for his unfaithfulness. Or in the case of a person who has been deeply wounded by another, so that he is full of bitterness toward the offender, the Lord sometimes chooses to reveal to him the sinfulness of his own response to the offense that was given. This revelation often breaks through the anger, reveals his self-righteousness for what it is, and leads him to forgive the one who offended him. In cases such as these, we judge wrongly based on a partial understanding of the situation – until God reveals to us other factors of which we are ignorant. For this reason, only God is truly qualified to judge, for He always understands fully our individual situations. He knows all the factors that lead to particular actions and responses, so He always judges justly. Therefore we can surrender judgment of others into His hands with the confidence that He will do what is right. As Willard correctly observes, "I can trust Jesus to go into the temple and drive out those who were profiting from religion, beating them with a rope. I cannot trust myself to do so."[7]

It is helpful here to look closely at the example of the Lord Jesus. The actions taken against Him by the crowds, the Jewish leaders, and the Roman authorities were clearly unjust. There was no basis for the charges against Him, much less the awful sentence of crucifixion. Yet He did not revile them, He did not judge them, and He did not call down the angels of God to destroy them. Rather, He quietly asked God to forgive them, and then gave up His spirit for all of mankind. How did He do that? The Apostle Peter explains:

When they hurled their insults at him, he did not retaliate;
when he suffered, he made no threats. Instead, he entrusted
himself to him who judges justly.

(1 Peter 2:23)

That's the secret to staying within the realm of godly discernment. We leave judgment in God's hands, for we know that
only He can judge accurately the thoughts and intentions of a
person's heart. This does not mean that we do not recognize
the injustice of another's actions toward us, if indeed they have
acted unjustly. It doesn't mean that we pretend everything is
OK when it isn't. Rather, we offer that injustice up to God and
trust that He will make things right in His time. Of course, His
timing may not line up exactly with ours, but we can be
confident that in the end He will "judge justly."

One of the biggest challenges we face as believers is
discerning when we are using godly discernment in our
relationships with others and when we have fallen into the
trap of judging them. It is my hope that these eight questions
will help others, just as I have found them helpful in my own
life. Of course, not every question will be helpful in every
situation. Sometimes, for example, questions 1 and 3 will be
most helpful, while in other cases questions 2 and 6 will bring
the most clarity to the situation. What is most important is to
consider prayerfully all the questions and to open up our
hearts to the Spirit's leading. He will certainly show us where
we are walking in godliness and where we have stepped
outside of God's plan for our lives by making ungodly
judgments. These judgments can take various forms, including some of the types of judgments that we will discuss in the
following chapter.

Diagnostic Questions for Ungodly Judgments

Diagnostic question:	*Key scripture:*
1. Would we feel comfortable if they viewed and evaluated us in the same way we are evaluating them?	"So in everything, do to others what you would have them do to you, for this sums up the Law and the Prophets." (Matthew 7:12)
2. Are we giving proper attention to their strengths as well as their weaknesses?	"Why do you look [continuously] at the speck of sawdust in your brother's eye ... ?" (Matthew 7:3)
3. Are we developing "spiritual far-sightedness"?	"Why do you look at the speck of sawdust in your brother's eye and pay no attention to the plank in your own eye?" (Matthew 7:3)
4. Are we hoping, believing, and praying that they can change for the better?	It [love] always protects, always trusts, always hopes, always perseveres. (1 Corinthians 13:7)
5. Are we evaluating their behavior rather than speculating about their hidden motives and intentions?	Therefore judge nothing before the appointed time; wait till the Lord comes. He will bring to light what is hidden in darkness and will expose the motives of men's hearts. (1 Corinthians 4:5)
6. Do we regard them as brothers and sisters in Christ rather than looking down on them because of their sins and their shortcomings?	For this very reason, Christ died and returned to life so that he might be the Lord of both the dead and the living. You, then, why do you judge your brother? Or why do you look down on your brother? (Romans 14:9–10)
7. Are we discriminating against certain groups of people?	My brothers, as believers in our glorious Lord Jesus Christ, don't show favoritism ... If you show special attention to the man wearing fine clothes ... have you not discriminated among yourselves and become judges with evil thoughts? (James 2:1–4)

Diagnostic Questions for Ungodly Judgments (*cont.*)

Diagnostic question:	*Key scripture:*
8. Are we consciously choosing to leave judgment in God's hands?	There is only one Lawgiver and Judge, the one who is able to save and destroy. But you –who are you to judge your neighbor? (James 4:12)

Notes

1. The importance of this distinction is discussed briefly in Dallas Willard, *The Divine Conspiracy* (London: Fount Paperbacks, 1998), 247–249.

2. D.A. Carson, *The Sermon on the Mount* (Carlisle, UK: Paternoster Press, 1978), 115.

3. The concept of "bearing with one another" implies that other believers often have faults and shortcomings that are difficult for them to correct or overcome. When we "bear with" other Christians, we choose to love them in spite of their shortcomings. We do this because it is the Lord's will for us, and because they are precious in His sight.

4. The parallelism between *blepeis* in the first clause and *katanoeis* in the second, as well as the use of the present tense in both cases, suggests that the emphasis is on the continuous nature of the attention we give to the faults of others. We can truly become fixated on or obsessed with the sins and faults of others. Cf. Alfred Plummer, *A Critical and Exegetical Commentary on the Gospel according to S. Luke*, 5th edn (Edinburgh: T & T Clark, 1922), 191, who writes that the word *katanoeis* "expresses prolonged attention and observation."

5. As Willard points out, " 'Getting the board out' is not a matter of correcting something that is wrong in our life so that we will be able to condemn our dear ones better – more effectively, so to speak." Rather, "condemnation *is* the board in our eye" (247, emphasis added).

6. It is important to note that these matters are not specifically commanded or prohibited by the Lord Himself or by the teaching of the apostles. Now that the Bible is complete, the critical issue would be whether the matter at hand was specifically commanded or prohibited in Scripture.

7. Willard, 243.

Chapter 3

Types of
Ungodly Judgments

Some years ago I counseled with a young man who was struggling with his sexuality. Though he was a committed believer, he had been involved sexually with each of a series of girlfriends, including the young woman he was currently dating. He realized his behavior was not pleasing to God and desired to repent of it, but he was surprised at the power sexual sin had in his life. He was having trouble breaking free of it on his own, so we began tracing out the roots of his problem.

As we talked, it became clear that this young man had a strong prejudice – actually a judgment – against another people group in Indonesia. This judgment arose because he felt his father had been treated unfairly by his superiors, most of whom were from this people group. I then asked about his past girlfriends and found that most of them were from the people group he had judged so harshly. At that point I understood the deepest roots of his struggle. It became clear that his tendency toward sexual sin had come not merely from raging hormones and the urgings of the flesh, but also from a desire for revenge. By taking the virginity and the honor of young women from that people group, he was seeking to pay back the group for what they had done to his father. His involvement in sexual sin was, at least in part, the outworking of the judgment he had made in his heart. For that reason, I led him in forgiving the members of that people group, in renouncing the judgment he had made against them, and in breaking the power of the judgment in his life. Dealing with the judgment that was at the root of his sexual issues was essential if he was to repent once for all of the sinful, destructive pattern in which he was involved.

Judgments can influence our lives in different and varied ways. This is due to the fact that judgments come in various types. In fact, judgments vary as to their nature, their object, and their impact in a person's life. Some influence only the believer's relationship with the person who is the object of the judgment, while other types of judgments influence virtually every aspect of a person's life. We need to be aware of several types of judgments that often take root in the lives of believers. Only then can we guard ourselves from falling into these traps, and so walk in the freedom and abundant life that God desires for His children.

Judgments against God

After counseling hundreds of people, mostly Christians, it is still amazing to me how many have made judgments against God at some point in their lives.[1] These are often made in times of difficulty, trauma, or abuse when God seems distant or does not seem to answer their repeated calls for help. To some it seems that God does not exist, or if He does, that He really does not care about them or their needs. Based on that conclusion, which is really a judgment, they deduce that it is futile to bring their concerns to God in prayer. This type of judgment quickly undermines their relationship with their heavenly Father.

Many of us have been tempted to fall into this type of judgment. I still recall with clarity the events of 1994 when we had just made the move from Bowling Green, Kentucky, to Bandung, West Java. After less than six months on the field we received word that my mother-in-law Elinor's cancer, which had been in remission for some time, was now in a critical – and probably terminal – stage. We quickly made arrangements to return to the States to have some time with her and then left again for the field after a wonderful month together. At that point she was fairly stable and being treated aggressively by a well-known oncologist, so we felt we should return to our language study in Indonesia.

Elinor was a wonderful woman and our kids loved her dearly, in spite of the distance that separated us. They were all praying fervently for their grandma and, of course, Katy and I were interceding with them. After some weeks, however, her condition worsened, and it seemed that she would soon be with her Lord. The rest of us began to accept the fact that Elinor was going to experience the perfect healing that comes only when we are with Jesus, but our oldest son, Chris, who was ten at the time, continued to pray in faith that God would heal his grandma. I still remember the day before Elinor's death Chris said to me, "You know, Dad, Grandma still has a 50 percent chance of being healed. It's up to God whether she's healed or not."

When Elinor went home to be with the Lord it was hard for all of us, and there were tears all around. Several weeks later, however, I saw the results of Elinor's death in Chris' life. He was facing a difficult situation at that time, and we encouraged him to take the matter to the Lord in prayer. He looked thoughtful for a moment, and then he said, "I don't know. I prayed about Grandma and look what happened." The seeds of a judgment against God were sown in his heart, so Katy and I spent a lot of time talking to him about God's love and how sometimes His plan for our lives is different than our own. We told him that God's plan is not always easy, but He always desires the best for us as His children.

We must take care not to make judgments against God when we're in the midst of trials and afflictions. However, not all judgments against God begin there. Some people generalize from experiences with their own fathers. Since, for example, their fathers were unfaithful and never kept a promise, some believers conclude that their heavenly Father is also untrustworthy. If their own fathers were absent from the home physically or emotionally, other people tend to regard their heavenly Father in the same way. People whose fathers were perfectionists – impossible to please – often feel that nothing they do is acceptable to God. These believers create their own concept of God apart from the teachings of Scripture, and they do so in their fathers' image. Of course, logically it makes no sense to base our conception of God's character on our negative experience with our earthly father, but who says judgments have to be logical?

The interesting thing about judgments against God is that they can influence our relationship with Him long after they are forgotten. This is one reason some believers are unable to experience intimacy with their heavenly Father, even though intellectually they know that He loves them deeply. At some point in their life, perhaps when they were still a child, they made a judgment against God. In time, however, this judgment was forgotten. They began to study the Bible and to attend a solid, Bible-believing church. They grew in their understanding of God's love, but somehow they could not connect with Him in their private devotions or in public worship. The intimacy they desired with the heavenly Father seemed to elude them, leaving them frustrated and longing for a deeper experience of God's love. Why do some believers struggle in this way? Often they struggle because the judgment they once made is still at work deep within their heart. They may believe intellectually that God loves them unreservedly, but they are unable to experience His love at a deep level. Somehow their head and their heart are in conflict.

When we judge God, not only are we sinning against Him, but we are putting up a barrier that will keep us from experiencing the joy of intimacy with Him. Indeed, judgments against God cut us off from the very source of our spiritual life and strength. That is why this type of judgment is such a powerful tool in the Enemy's hand. He will attempt to utilize many experiences to lead us into making ungodly judgments against God. In the midst of these experiences, he may suggest that God does not love us, that God will not answer our prayers, or he may deceive us in many other ways. That is his part in the process. In the end, however, we ourselves are the ones who decide whether we embrace the deception, whether we make a judgment against God or not. Therefore, we must be alert and watchful, especially in the midst of trials and afflictions, so we do not fall into this trap.

Judgments against ourselves

Many people, including many Christians, have labeled themselves in negative ways, and so make ungodly and unhealthy judgments against themselves. In some cases, the judgments are completely false, while in other cases they contain an element of truth, but lack balance and overshadow the person's positive characteristics. There is a subtle distinction here that is critical to understanding the nature of ungodly judgments. The fact is we all have limitations, and accepting our limitations is a sign of maturity. Yet defining ourselves only in terms of our limitations is self-defeating. That is precisely what we do when we make judgments against ourselves.

Self-judgments can take different forms. Sometimes these labels relate to a person's character. They see themselves, for example, as "difficult," "stubborn," or "rebellious," and for the most part they live out the judgment they have made on themselves.

Other times judgments relate to a person's appearance, so

that they view themselves as "homely," "fat," or just plain "ugly." This kind of self-judgment can impact a person's self-image to the point that it defines who they are. An overweight person may have much to commend them in terms of personality, ability, and appearance, but the judgment they has made against themselves controls their thinking to the point that all they see in the mirror is a person who is "fat."

In other cases self-judgments relate to a person's intelligence or competence. Some people have heard so many times that they are "stupid," "ignorant," or "incompetent" that they see themselves primarily in those terms. Others embrace their parent's pronouncement that they will "never amount to anything." This kind of judgment can influence negatively their future prospects, in spite of the fact that they have natural intelligence and ability.

In certain cases self-judgments relate to our status before God, as when a person believes the lie that they are "unworthy of being loved," "wicked," or "dirty," often because of past sin or abuse. In spite of scriptural evidence to the contrary, they embrace the lies that originated from the false assertions of others, their own incorrect interpretation of their past experiences, or the suggestions of demonic powers. In the end, this type of judgment usually disrupts the development of the person's relationship with God and with other people, and brings tremendous pain into their lives.

One young woman who received ministry illustrates this kind of judgment. As a small child she had experienced sexual abuse at the hands of an older relative and was struggling to overcome the impact of that abuse in her life. She shared that she was often hard on herself. If she made a small mistake, she would be haunted and overwhelmed by the feeling that she had committed a great wrong. Her feelings were frequently out of proportion to the mistake that she had made, so we knew we should look for a deeper cause, probably related to the abuse she had experienced.

As we prayed for her, the Lord revealed the root of her feelings. She had embraced the idea that she was "wrong" for not thwarting the relative's attempt to abuse her sexually. In her mind she knew that it was unrealistic to think that as a small child she could repel the advances of an older and much stronger relative, but in her heart she felt that there must have been something she could have done. Once we identified the deception and the self-judgment, we asked God to show us His truth that would set her free. Immediately another memory surfaced. She could see herself as a young teen, who for some reason had to spend the night at this relative's home. In the memory, she saw herself moving all the furniture in the bedroom in front of the door so that no one – especially this relative – could enter while she slept. At that moment the light went on in her understanding. She said, "I know what the Lord is showing me! When I was old enough, I did do something to stop my relative. But when he abused me, I was just too small." We led her in prayer to confess this truth to the Lord and broke the power of her self-judgment. After that session, she experienced a marked decrease in her tendency to be hard on herself for small mistakes. Of course, there were a number of other areas in her life that required prayer ministry as well, but breaking the power of this self-judgment was a major breakthrough for her.

Judgments against ourselves may have an element of truth in them, which makes them all the more dangerous and potentially destructive. A child may tend toward rebellion as he deals with a difficult situation at home by expressing his innate tendency toward sin and disobedience. Then, as a result of his rebellion, he is judged and labeled by his parents, teachers, and other significant adults in his life. If he embraces this judgment and turns it against himself, he will likely continue down the road of increasing rebellion until such a time as he is set free from the power of the judgment of others and the self-judgment he has made against himself.

Judgments against others

Most of the passages in the New Testament that address the topic of ungodly judgments refer to judgments we make against other people, especially our brothers and sisters in Christ. Why is this? I believe it is because people have an inherited sinful tendency to judge their fellow human beings. This can be true for both Christians and non-Christians. In fact, in my experience Christians can be some of the most judgmental people on the face of the planet! This is especially true if they adhere to a strict moral code that includes both biblical prohibitions and extra-biblical additions based on their church's tradition. Such a code is designed to keep them walking in holiness and obedience to Christ, but it can easily become the basis on which they judge others. They can forget that everything from their adoption as God's children to their growth and progress in sanctification is due to God's unmerited favor. They can lose a sense of love and compassion for people who do not yet know Jesus, who have not yet grown in certain areas of their lives, or who are mature in Christ but see certain issues in a different way. If that happens, judging others is frequently the result.

There are three types of judgments against others that differ in their nature and impact in a person's life, namely individual judgments, generalizing judgments, and judgments against parents. In addition, we must pause to consider the concept of "bitter-root judgments" as it has been developed in the writings of John and Paula Sandford. These types of judgments are similar in certain respects, but there are enough differences that we must consider them separately in this section.

Individual judgments
If we were to speak of a "simple" type of judgment, this is it. Individual judgments are made against another person and tend to influence primarily the life of the one making the judgment, the life of the one who is being judged, and the

relationship between these two parties. There may be some truth in the judgment that is made about the person, but it also lacks balance, ignores the person's positive characteristics, and is harsh and critical in spirit.[2] Therefore, "simple" judgments against others are sinful in God's sight.

If we are not careful, we can fall into the trap of making these kinds of judgments against almost anyone. Husbands can make judgments against their wives and vice versa. In fact, in marital counseling we often find that the root of a couple's problems is the judgment that one partner has made against the other. In some cases, married people even have affairs due at least in part to the ungodly judgments that they have made against their spouse. For example, a husband's judgment against his wife often colors his perceptions of her, so that he forgets about all her positive qualities and becomes obsessed with her negative traits. At the same time, however, he is relating to other women at work, at the health club, and even at church whom he has not judged . . . yet! Because his perception of them is not influenced by a judgment against them, they seem so much more appealing than his wife, and in many cases one thing leads to another.

Parents can also fall into the trap of judging their children, which can have devastating effects in the lives of their kids. These judgments often relate to their appearance (e.g. "My second son is fat"), their personality ("My oldest daughter is just plain rebellious"), or their potential in life ("My boy will never amount to anything"). Once the judgment is made, it colors subsequent interactions between the parent and the child, so that the message of the judgment is driven home again and again. The judgment can lodge in the heart of the child, wounding her deeply and creating low self-esteem, while at the same time influencing her expectations of herself and her openness to new opportunities and challenges. In the end, the odds are fairly high that she will turn out pretty much as her parents expected.[3]

Children can also make judgments against their parents. If the parents are not skilled relationally, their interactions can leave their children feeling unvalued or misunderstood. At that point, the child may embrace the judgment that his father is a "jerk," that he "only cares about himself," or that he "never understands." This type of judgment can lead ultimately to a further breakdown in the parent-child relationship, with the result that virtually everything the parent says or does is interpreted in a negative light. This is especially common in the teen years, but can also happen earlier in a child's life. Dealing effectively with judgments against parents is a critical element in effective prayer counseling and will be dealt with in detail later in this chapter.

Judgments can also take place in the church, as when believers judge their pastor or other church leaders, or the pastor makes judgments against members of his congregation. These kinds of judgments can take place in almost any situation or relationship. In fact, after six years of ministry experience as a pastor and thirteen years as a missionary, I have come to believe that these judgments are very common among God's people, due at least in part to the absence of biblical teaching on the subject that is practical and systematic. I believe that many church problems and splits occur because of judgments that one person or group has made against another. Frequently, people develop an "us–them" mentality based around a judgment that they have made on another faction in the church, which leads to further conflict and division. For example, members who love to sing traditional hymns often regard those who prefer modern praise songs as "shallow," while the other faction – which is composed of those who love to sing contemporary music – frequently view the hymn-singers as "spiritually dead." In the end, the outworking of this judgment is division. The opposing factions spend more time pushing their agenda than they do worshiping God.

One interesting thing about "simple" judgments is that they

often grow and develop over time. Once we have judged another person, we tend to interpret most of their words and actions in a negative way; that is, in accordance with the judgment that we have made against them. Often we ascribe negative motivations to them as well. It is as if we are viewing them through a negative filter. Our negative interpretations of their words and their actions then work, in turn, to strengthen the judgment against them. We become caught in a vicious cycle and often distance ourselves from the person, limiting our interaction with them to a bare minimum. That distance gives our imagination free reign to develop negative thoughts and fantasies about the person in line with the ever-deepening judgment that we have made against them. After some time our perspective on the person can be anything but objective.

Several years ago the Lord convicted Katy and me that we had made a judgment against another missionary couple. We had observed some negative characteristics in the life of this couple, had slapped a judgment on them, and then began interpreting everything they said and did in light of that judgment. Our imaginations really began working overtime!

After the Lord convicted us of our sin, we repented of the judgment we had made against them and asked Him to help us love this couple. After that, it was amazing to see the Lord work. Both Katy and I found ourselves involved in ministries with them and as a result came to know them better. Over time we observed their many fine qualities, as well as their effect-iveness in the Lord's work, and both of us came to respect them deeply. I am sure they still have some faults – all of us do – but their weaknesses no longer dominate the way we think and feel about them. The power of the judgment we made against them is broken.

Generalizing judgments

This type of judgment can have a devastating impact on the life of the one who is sitting as judge. Often it begins with a simple judgment against another person such as an abusive parent, an unfaithful husband, or an offensive person of a different race or nationality. Then, based on a negative experience with that person, the individual making the judgment generalizes to the point that the person they have judged represents a larger group of people. This larger group can be defined on the basis of gender (e.g. "all men" or "all women"), marital status (e.g. "all husbands" or "all wives"), race (e.g. "all Asians" or "all Hispanics"), nationality (e.g. "all Americans" or "all Japanese"), or even denominational affiliation (e.g. "all Baptists," "all Pentecostals," or "all Evangelicals"), as well as a host of other criteria. If a person is a member of one of these groups, then they automatically come under judgment. All the negative characteristics that are attributed to the group are uncritically attributed to the individual. That is the way generalizing judgments typically work.

One often sees the negative impact of this type of judgment in the lives of counselees. A very common scenario is when a little girl has an indifferent or abusive father and then is wounded or abused by several other men in her life such as her grandfather, brother, or boyfriend. Often she begins by making a judgment on one of the men who has wounded her, but this judgment can quickly generalize to the point that she distrusts and expects the worst from any man. In some cases she will attempt to protect herself by distancing herself from men. Often she will delay marriage or, if she is married, will find that true intimacy is impossible due to the protective barriers she has erected based on the judgment she has made in her heart.

In other cases the impact of the judgment against men is very different. It can become a self-fulfilling prophecy so that a woman experiences a series of unsatisfying or abusive relationships with men. It is amazing how often we encounter this particular pattern in counseling. A woman reports being abused as a child by a close relative, in some cases her own father, and then is treated poorly by other men who are close to her. This may be a cousin, an uncle, a neighbor, a family friend, or even her own brother. This kind of treatment often prompts the victim to make a judgment against men in general. When she becomes a young woman, she then moves in and out of relationships with men who treat her poorly or even abusively. These unsatisfying relationships only serve to reinforce her initial judgment against men, and so the bondage deepens.

Why do we see this pattern over and over again? Clearly a woman's self-image is a major factor. In some cases abuse victims feel that they do not deserve better, or that "decent" guys (if, indeed, there is such a person!) would not be interested in them. Such feelings are often the result of the shame of sexual abuse. In other cases, they may be trying to punish themselves. Then, of course, there's the expectation that guys will abuse them, which can become self-fulfilling. Certainly these factors are critical in many cases.

After counseling many women who have fallen into this trap, however, I believe there is more to this pattern of abuse, at least in some cases. Why is this? First, the psychological factors I have listed above do not explain fully the frequency with which we encounter this pattern, nor do they help us understand the strength of the bondage in a woman's life. Second, this type of life pattern typically involves several factors that can give the Enemy an opportunity to work in a person's life. In addition to the trauma of abuse, there is also the deep-level deception that results from this experience (e.g. "No decent man would want me"). Then there's the bitterness that usually results from such treatment, as well as the ungodly judgment and the negative expectation that all men will treat her poorly. All these factors give the Enemy an opportunity to deepen the bondage in a woman's life.

We have all known victims of abuse who continue to be drawn into abusive relationships. Given what we know about Satan's strategies, it would not be surprising if demonic powers are at work in a woman's life as a result of her past traumas and her responses to those experiences. These powers appear to attract men – also probably demonized – who have a tendency toward abusiveness, bringing further trouble and abuse into her life. Over time this deepens the impact on her self-image as well as strengthening her bitterness toward men and the judgment she has made against them. As always, the Enemy is ready to press his advantage to the fullest by deepening the level of bondage in a person's life.[4]

I have focused on a particular example of a generalizing judgment to show how it can lead us into bondage. However, judgments by women against men are by no means the only type of generalizing judgment that we encounter in counseling. Men also judge the opposite sex based on negative or traumatic experiences with certain women. I have counseled young men who were not at all interested in attractive women because of traumatic experiences with their mother, or after a particularly traumatic experience with a former girlfriend. It is not that their orientation is homosexual. They simply have no interest in having a romantic relationship with women. Judgments of this type can ultimately prevent people from marrying, or hinder intimacy between husband and wife within the context of marriage.

Judgments against people of one's own gender can also play an important role in the development of gender confusion, homosexual tendencies, or even a "gay" lifestyle. A boy's relationship with a father who is harsh and abusive or even distant and unengaged can leave him with a distorted sense of what is masculine, thus creating a deep-rooted ambivalence toward people of his own gender. On the one hand, he will grow up craving the kind of masculine love and affirmation that he should have received from his father, while on the other hand he will "split off from the masculine," to quote Mario Bergner.[5] Bergner describes the beginnings of this process in his own life as follows:

Unlike many children, I never wanted to imitate my father because I never saw in him qualities I admired. Not only did he fail to affirm me as a man, through emotional abuse he denigrated my emerging masculinity. So I repressed my masculinity, simply detaching from all that my father literally was to me. I actually remember making an inner vow never to become like him.

This vow and detachment from my father eventually generalized to all that he represented to me, including all other men. In my deep heart or inner being, my personality became split off from symbols of masculinity altogether.[6]

At the root of this "splitting off" is a judgment against his father, which generalizes to the point that it becomes a judgment against all that is masculine. This leads to an "inner vow" that widens the split with his own gender.[7] These early seeds of a judgment against the masculine can, in some cases, crystallize during Junior High and High School, when the person longs to be like the athletes and other "manly men," but is instead mocked and rejected by them. In the end, due to his rejection of the masculine, he does not experience a normal attraction to women as "other" and "complementary." Distanced in this way from both the masculine and the feminine, his legitimate need for healthy male affection can become sexualized. In that case, he may turn to homosexual relationships to provide what he should have received in the context of normal relationships with both men and women.

As we can see from these examples, judgments can generalize in a variety of ways. The interesting thing about this type of judgment, however, is the way they control our perceptions of others. We tend to see the people we are judging in a negative light, as if we are wearing dark glasses. We become virtually obsessed with their faults, shortcomings, and sins – "the specks in their eyes." When, however, we forgive the people who have hurt us and repent of the judgment we have made against them and the group they represent, often our perceptions change dramatically. I have listened to counselees share in amazement how things have changed since they repented of the judgments that were influencing their thoughts, feelings, and perceptions. People and groups they thought were evil and unworthy of their trust are now seen in a different light, and they are able to appreciate their positive traits and the gifts and talents that God has entrusted to them.

One counselee, a young woman, came from a particularly dysfunctional home in which abusive ways of relating to each other had become the norm. Her defense in the midst of this difficult environment had been to make a particularly nasty judgment against all of humanity, and to keep her distance from other people. The fundamental deception at the root of the judgment was that all people were like the members of her family: they would hurt you if given half a chance. As we talked through her relational difficulties, she came to realize that the judgment she had made on others – her fleshly defense against further pain and rejection – was actually a liability. Not only was it sinful, but it was undermining her relationships with others. We led her in confessing and rejecting the judgment, then prayed to break the power of the judgment in her life. On that day she experienced a powerful deliverance. I still remember her words to me the following week. She exclaimed in amazement, "I'm like a stranger to myself! I used to think of my co-workers so negatively, but now I see that they're really good people. What has happened to me?" The answer to her question was simple: the deceptive power of the judgment had been broken, and she could now see others more objectively and recognize their strengths as well as their weaknesses.

Judgments against parents

Why place judgments against parents in a class by itself? There are three reasons behind this decision. First, there is the frequency with which we encounter this type of judgment.

Many people who come from abusive and dy
homes fall into this trap. Instead of experiencing
support, they have been neglected, criticized,
abused, and rejected by their parents. Therefore, from
point of view, it is completely understandable if they choose to
judge their parents, to reject them, and to harbor bitterness and
hatred against them all their days. In fact, many people do
respond to their parents' sin in precisely these ways. Nevertheless, the cross of Christ calls us to entrust ourselves to Him
who judges justly. We must forgive our parents and release the
judgments we have made in our hearts against them. We must
choose to love and honor our parents in spite of their sins and
shortcomings, just as Christ loves us and accepts us in spite of
our faults and our transgressions. Only then can we experience
true freedom and victory in Christ.

Second, there is the fact that judgments against parents
violate a basic principle of God's Word that is stated plainly
in the Old Testament (Exodus 20:12; Deuteronomy 5:16),
reiterated by Jesus Himself in the gospels (Matthew 15:4;
19:19), and emphasized by the Apostle Paul in the letter to the
Ephesians, namely that children are to honor their parents:

> "Honor your father and mother" – which is the first com-
> mandment with a promise – "that it may go well with you and
> that you may enjoy long life on the earth."
>
> (Ephesians 6:2)

The connection between the command and the promise is
critical to a proper understanding of the impact of judgments
against parents. The basic principle is that when we who have
given our lives to Jesus Christ choose to honor our parents,
usually things "go well" with us. On the other hand, since
judging one's parents is antithetical to honoring them, this type
of judgment frequently blocks the flow of God's blessings into
a person's life, particularly spiritual blessings such as joy and

peace. Ultimately, the choice is ours. However, many believers are unaware of the impact of this type of judgment on their lives and ministries, and so do not repent of them and break their power. The consequences can be tragic.

Third, because they tend to generalize in a variety of ways, judgments against parents can be devastating in their impact on the relationships between the children who make them and people who later happen to play a role in their lives. Judgments can influence the person's relationships with a variety of adults who are like their parents in some respects. For example, if a parent tends to be authoritarian in her parenting style, her child may experience difficulty in following a leader whose has a similar style. The child might become critical of the leader's faults and fall into the trap of judging him. These judgments can also influence dramatically the relationship between the child and his or her spouse, particularly if the spouse is like the parent in some respects.

Several observations can help us understand the uniqueness of judgments against parents. For one thing, these judgments are often implicit in nature and express themselves in the making of informal vows. For example, a person may react to their parents' relational style by saying, "I'm not going to treat my wife like my dad treats my mom!", or "I'm not going to be a parent like my parents!" Even though these statements are made in the form of a vow, they are based on an implicit judgment against the parents, e.g. "Dad was a real jerk of a husband," or "My parents were horrible." Once again, there may be some truth in these statements, but they lack balance, ignore the parent's positive characteristics, and demonstrate a harshness of spirit that is inappropriate in a believer's life. Ultimately such judgments are dishonoring to their parents and displeasing to the Lord.[8]

This kind of implicit judgment often leads believers away from following Christ in the power of the Holy Spirit. A Christian man, for example, should seek out God's will for his relationship with his wife and children in the Scriptures and ask the Holy Spirit to help him become a godly husband or father. If, however, he has made a judgment on his father and taken an inner vow that he will not become a husband and father like his dad, his orientation will be very different. He will focus his effort on not becoming like his father in his relationship with his wife and children. His reference point will not be Christ and His will for his life and family, but rather his father's relationship with his wife and their children, against which he is reacting with great determination. Since his efforts are based upon an ungodly judgment, his efforts will not be Spirit-led and Spirit-empowered. He will forge ahead in his own strength, which often leads to failure. Some people end up at the opposite extreme from their father, while others end up becoming a husband or father who is very much like him. Once again, the destructive power of judgments, as well as the vows that often grow out of them, should not be underestimated.

"Bitter-root judgments and expectations"

No treatment of ungodly judgments would be complete without some discussion of the concept of "bitter-root judgments," which was popularized by John and Paula Sandford back in 1979.[9] The influence of their writings on this subject is obvious if we search the Internet using the words "bitter-root judgments." The websites of church-based counseling ministries all over the country, as well as many professional counseling services, mention the importance of breaking the power of these judgments in a counselee's life. It is obvious that many people have benefited greatly from their writings, both personally and in their counseling ministry. And I myself have learned much from their various publications, as I mentioned earlier. Nevertheless, it is important that we evaluate the biblical and logical basis of their teachings on this type of judgment before applying these principles in our lives and our ministries.

The nature of "bitter-root judgments and expectations"

What exactly are "bitter-root judgments"? According to the Sandfords' explanation, these judgments are made against one's parents during childhood. The impact of the judgment is not immediately evident, however. It may lie dormant for years, until the time for "reaping" arrives. At that point the results in a person's life, and the impact on their marriage, can be devastating. The tiny seed of the judgment that they have sown will, inevitably, cause them to reap a "whirlwind." They will find themselves acting irrationally, and their judgment will even "defile" their marriage partner, thus creating destructive patterns in their lives.

The Sandfords give several examples of "bitter-root judgments" and share a testimony of how they experienced the power of this principle both in their counseling ministry and in their own lives and marriage. One example was about a couple named Burt and Martha. Their presenting problem was that Martha was overweight, and Burt was constantly criticizing her regarding her weight. Her husband's criticism left Martha stressed and feeling worse about herself, which led her to eat more and to gain more weight. This, of course, brought forth more criticism from Burt, and so the cycle continued.

The Sandfords' conclusion was that "bitter-root judgments" were at the heart of their problems. Burt's mother was obese and slovenly, and he had judged her for her appearance and her lifestyle. "His bitter root judgment and consequent expectation was that his wife would become obese and slovenly."[10] Martha, on the other hand, had grown up with a father whom she could never please, no matter how hard she tried, and had judged him for his critical spirit. "Her bitter root judgment and expectancy was that the man of her life would always be critical of her; she would never be acceptable or be able to be pleasing to her man."[11]

Their marriage began well. Martha was slim and beautiful, and Bert was able to compliment her sincerely on her appearance. Then the time for "reaping" arrived. Martha gained some weight as a result of her pregnancy, and Burt began to scold her and to criticize her for her appearance. Though both of them were unaware of the "bitter-root judgments" they had made as children, they were reaping precisely what they had sown. Their judgments were literally "defiling" their marriage partners, so that Martha became obese and Burt became critical. They had sown a small judgment, but because of the fact that the judgment dishonored their parents, they were reaping tremendous consequences in their marriage. As the Sandfords write, "We sow a spark and reap a forest fire, or sow to the wind and reap whirlwind."[12]

The importance of the concept of "bitter-root judgments" in the Sandfords' ministry is illustrated in the following paragraph:

> Burt and Martha are not unique. We have found bitter-root judgments and expectancies in every couple we counsel! Bitter-root judgments are the most common, most basic sins in all marital relationships – perhaps in all of life. These three simple laws affect all life: 1) Life will go well for us in every area in which we could in fact honor our parents and life will not go well in every area in which we could not honor them; 2) We will receive harm in the same areas of life in which we have meted out judgment against others; 3) We will most surely reap what we have sown. We regard these laws as the most powerful keys God has revealed to His people for the healing of relationships. These three laws are the basis of almost all our counseling.[13]

We must bear in mind that this paradigm has been adopted and utilized by many churches and counseling ministries around the world. For that reason, it is critical that we understand as accurately as possible the concept of "bitter-root judgments and expectations" so that we can evaluate the concept in light of the teachings of Scripture.

The biblical basis for "bitter-root judgments and expectations"
In the ministry of counseling and inner healing, we must continually return to the Scriptures for guidance and direction. Otherwise, we can lose balance in our perspective and our teaching, or even develop concepts and paradigms that lack biblical support or are antithetical to the teaching of Scripture.

When we examine the biblical basis of "bitter-root judgments and expectations," several aspects of the concept require comment. First, there is the matter of the name, which is based on Hebrews 12:15,

> See to it that no-one misses the grace of God and that no bitter root grows up to cause trouble and defile many.

If we examine the verse in its broader context, however, it is clear that it refers to those who lose heart under persecution and turn away from the Christian faith. They are the "bitter root" that "grows up to cause trouble and defile many," presumably by leading them into sin and apostasy. I can state with confidence that verse 15 does not refer to judgments we make as children against our parents that later "defile" our marriage partner. Such an interpretation is completely foreign to the context of Hebrews chapter 12.

Second, there is the Sandfords' frequent reference to the fifth commandment (Exodus 20:12), which is quoted and re-emphasized in the teaching of Jesus and the apostles. The citations in Jesus' teaching are brief, but the Apostle Paul utilizes the longer version in Ephesians 6:1–3:

> Children, obey your parents in the Lord, for this is right.
> "Honor your father and mother" – which is the first

commandment with a promise – "that it may go well with you and that you may enjoy long life on the earth."[14]

The Sandfords' interpretation of this command and the accompanying promise is evident in the following passage from *The Transformation of the Inner Man*: "When Burt judged his mother, the law which declares that the measure he metes out he must receive, went into effect. When his judgment dishonored his mother ... that meant that Deuteronomy 5:16 ensured that life would not go well for him *in that regard*" (emphasis added).[15] The critical phrase that the Sandfords have added is "in that regard." In the context of their argument, these words mean that Burt's judgment as a child against his overweight mother virtually guaranteed that later his wife would suffer from a weight problem. Conversely, Martha's childish judgment against her father for his frequent criticism ensured that later her husband would become critical of her as well. The promise connected to the fifth command is that specific, at least according to the Sandfords' interpretation.

It is important to observe, however, that the words "in that regard" do not appear in any of the versions of the fifth commandment in either the Old or the New Testaments. Also, when we examine the context of the Deuteronomy 5:16 passage, the clause "that it may go well with you" means that those who honor their parents will experience the blessings of the covenant and avoid the curses for disobedience. In short, they will enjoy a life of divine blessing. There is certainly no indication in the verse or in its context that a specific judgment against a parent will later bring *the same problem* into the life of the person's spouse.

Third, the Sandfords' use of the concept of sowing and reaping deserves comment. In the Apostle Paul's writings this concept is used in at least two different ways, neither of which implies that we will reap *in precisely the area we have sown*. In 2 Corinthians 9:6–11 Paul utilizes this principle when he exhorts the church to participate generously in the collection for the poor saints in Judea. He reminds them boldly in verse 6:

> Remember this: Whoever sows sparingly will also reap sparingly, and whoever sows generously will also reap generously.

Of course, this does not mean that Christian stewardship is a kind of divine investment plan that is guaranteed to pay great financial dividends, though some teachers come close to this notion in their efforts to raise money for their ministries. If we look at the context of the verse, Paul writes that God will "make all grace abound to you" (v. 8), and that "You will be made rich in every way" (v. 11). The point is that those who give generously will be blessed richly with both the grace and the resources to give even more generously, resulting in thanksgiving to God. There is certainly no basis in this verse or its context to state that what we sow (especially as a child) we will *inevitably* reap "in the same regard or area of our life." While it is true that in some cases there is a connection between "reaping" and "sowing," so that there is a certain appropriateness in the consequences (e.g. a person who commits sexual sin [sowing] then contracts an STD [reaping]), this is not always the case.

The other passage where Paul uses the principle of reaping and sowing is in Galatians 6:7–9:

> Do not be deceived: God cannot be mocked. A man reaps what he sows. The one who sows to please his sinful nature, from that nature will reap destruction; the one who sows to please the Spirit, from the Spirit will reap eternal life. Let us not become weary in doing good, for at the proper time we will reap a harvest if we do not give up.

The principle is applied very simply in this passage. Depending on what we sow, we will reap one of two things: destruction or eternal life. Of course, this application of the principle of sowing and reaping does not exclude the possibility that specific actions will have specific temporal consequences. There is, however, no indication that a specific sin such as a judgment against parents will yield exactly the same thing in a person's life or the life of their spouse.

Fourth, the application of the principles of Matthew 7:1–2 and Luke 6:37–38 in the Sandfords' explanation of "bitter-root judgments and expectations" gives cause for concern. Clearly Matthew 7:1–2 refers to God's judgment at the end of the age,[16] though the Luke 6 passage is more ambiguous and could refer to a person's present experience as well as the end of the age:

> "Do not judge, and you will not be judged. Do not condemn, and you will not be condemned. Forgive, and you will be forgiven. Give, and it will be given to you. A good measure, pressed down, shaken together and running over, will be poured into your lap. For with the measure you use, it will be measured to you."

Once again, the context of these verses is critical to their proper interpretation. In Luke 6:27–36 Jesus has just exhorted both His disciples and the crowds to love even their enemies. "Be merciful, just as your Father is merciful" is His powerful conclusion to this section. Then He moves into some specific exhortations that are related to this theme of mercy. The point of these verses is that mercy toward others, whether it is expressed by withholding judgment, choosing not to condemn, or in forgiving the wrongs of others, will bring blessing into our lives.

There is nothing in these verses to indicate that judging another person (including a parent) will inevitably bring the *very characteristic we have judged in them* into our lives, or into the lives of our spouses. Instead, Jesus' teaching suggests that judging others will block the flow of God's blessings – in one form or another – into a person's life. The specific blessings that are forfeited could vary from case to case. For these reasons it is difficult to find here solid, biblical support for the concept of a "bitter-root judgment," at least as it is explained by the Sandfords.

Fifth, my final concern is more theological than biblical in nature. It relates to the impact of "bitter-root judgments" on another person's life. According to the Sandfords, these judgments function as follows:

> Since Burt had judged his mother for obesity, he was due to reap obesity – who would be a more likely person through whom to reap than his wife? His judgment helped first to draw to him a woman who was likely to have a weight problem; then it pushed Martha to gain weight. His necessity to reap what he had sown was therefore returning to him like a mighty wind. For Martha, that was like standing in a hundred-mile-an-hour gale, pushing her to fulfill his legal requirement by gaining weight.[17]

The overwhelming impact of these judgments is illustrated again later in the Sandfords' discussion, where they lament that many have misunderstood their teaching:

> We have learned to our chagrin that most who read or heard failed to grasp the point! They thought we were speaking only of psychological expectancy. In small part we were. Bitter-root expectancy is a psychological construct in our carnal natures by which we expect a self-fulfilling prophecy to happen, like always being criticized or rejected or left out of things. By it we do indeed coerce people or manipulate unconsciously until they do that bad thing to us which proves our judgment, "I knew it!" "I knew it would happen that way. It always does."

Such psychological expectancies do have some power in our lives. But compared to the laws of which we actually were speaking, psychological bitter-root expectancy is like a flickering candle flame beside an atomic blast! It is the Law of God which alone possesses limitless power![18]

One final quote is helpful as we attempt to understand fully the Sandfords' viewpoint. After emphasizing again and again that the law of sowing and reaping guarantees that "bitter-root judgments and expectations" will bring certain consequences into our lives, they put forth a small caveat:

Note the words, "...and by it the many be defiled" (Heb. 12:15). Our bitter root, by the force of reaping, actually defiles others. We *make* them act around us in ways they might successfully resist, apart from us...

We need to understand, however, that guilt is always fifty-fifty. Our bitter root could not overcome the other's free will unless something in him is still flesh (no matter how good and strong), or weak and sinful. The other is always responsible too. Guilt in a family is always shared.[19]

My concern with this teaching is that it is overly deterministic to the point that it undermines the responsibility of believers for their actions and their ability to walk in obedience by the power of the Holy Spirit. Could someone choose to live in godliness and holiness instead of succumbing to the destructive power that is at work in their life as a result of the judgment of another person with whom they are related? In spite of the caveat toward the end of the Sandfords' discussion, it seems doubtful whether any human being could actually do so, for they would have to resist the "limitless" power of God's law. The Sandfords do wish to maintain, however, that people are responsible for their actions, for the bitter root could not overcome a person's will "unless something in him is still flesh (no matter how good and strong) or weak and sinful." Yet this qualification means little since it is difficult to see how any human being could claim to be without weakness and sinful tendencies.[20] Ultimately, then, this teaching is deterministic in a way that is foreign to the New Testament, which commands us to relate to others in loving and godly ways in spite of their sin and the judgments that they have made against us and others. Wives are exhorted to submit to their unbelieving husbands, for example, in spite of the fact that they are still disobedient to the preaching of the gospel (e.g. 1 Peter 3:1–6). The ungodly judgments of others cannot be an excuse for our own inability or unwillingness to live in ways that are healthy and godly.

It is not my intention here to minimize the negative impact of ungodly judgments in a person's life. Nevertheless, as much as I appreciate the Sandfords' ministry, I do take issue with certain aspects of their teaching on bitter-root judgments. A number of general principles in Scripture are interpreted in a way that is foreign to their original context, and so are transformed into spiritual "laws" that determine quite specific- ally the consequences of our judgments. These "laws" are true both in the life of the person making the judgment and in the life of certain people who are closely related to them.

If we do not follow the Sandfords' teaching on bitter-root judgments, how do we explain the existence of cases such as Burt and Martha's? The explanation is relatively simple. From Burt's side, his sinful response to his mother's obesity and sloppiness was to make a vow that he would never marry a woman like his mother. Implicit in this vow was a judgment against her, which is linked to bitterness and unforgiveness. The result of the judgment and the accompanying vow is that "slimness" becomes all important to Burt, leading to a distortion of his system of values.

Everything goes well until Martha puts on some weight after her pregnancy. Her increased body mass triggers Burt's hyper-sensitivity to this issue. Instead of supporting his wife in her struggle to return to her pre-pregnancy weight, he instead becomes critical of her. "You're just like my mother" is a thought that recurs again and again in his mind, while his emotions alternate between shame and frustration/anger, precisely the feelings he experienced in his relationship with his mother. No doubt these thoughts and feelings emerge from the sinful judgment buried in his heart, but we must also allow for the influence of demonic powers. Certainly they are also at work to stimulate the thoughts and feelings that are destructive to Burt's life and marriage.

The anger and the judgment against his mother leaves Burt open to a multi-dimensional spiritual attack. He embraces the world's emphasis on outward appearance – particularly slimness – and thus judges his wife as inadequate based on her weight. He then expresses his dissatisfaction in a fleshly manner. Rather than encouraging and building up his wife and leaving her weight in the Lord's hands, he uses harsh criticism in an attempt to push her to lose weight. Of course, the results of this approach are disastrous. Finally, Burt's adoption of the world's values, as well as his fleshly attempts to push his wife into the world's mold, gives demonic powers an opportunity to work in his life, in Martha's life, and in their marriage relationship. Evil spirits remind Burt repeatedly of his wife's shortcoming, while at the same time they are reinforcing the impact of his critical words in Martha's life. This, of course, creates conflict and distance between them. Instead of building each other up in Christ, they are, quite literally, tearing each other apart.

Why are Burt and Martha in this situation? Is it because, according to God's "law," they must reap *in the same way that they have sown*? Was it, therefore, virtually inevitable that Burt would marry a woman who has a weight problem because he judged his mother for her weight? Was it also practically certain that Martha would marry a man who criticizes her because she judged her father because of his scathing criticisms of others? Scripture gives us no reason to believe that the principle of reaping and sowing can be interpreted and applied in such a rigid and narrow fashion. In some respects, of course, Burt and Martha are "reaping what they have sown." Instead of love, unity, and mutual support, their marriage has become a source of great misery for both of them. But there is no scriptural evidence to suggest that they are reaping a bitter harvest because the immutable power of God's law is forcing them to act the way they do.

My difference with the Sandfords is not that judgments against parents can have a devastating impact on people's lives and relationships. With that teaching I agree wholeheartedly. I believe, however, that such results come for different reasons. Clearly judging one's parents violates the command to honor them and thus sows seeds of destruction in a person's life. Also, when we harbor bitterness and resentment against our parents and judge them as lacking or unfit in some way, we open ourselves up to a multi-dimensional attack from the world, the flesh, and the devil. We react as the world reacts, we seek to establish our position through the efforts of the flesh, and we give an opportunity to demonic forces to influence our thoughts, our feelings, and our decisions. As always, if we give the Enemy an opportunity, he is ready to press his advantage.

In the context of marriage, Satan often seeks to play our weaknesses and our judgments against each other, as he did in the case of Burt and Martha. Martha's extra weight was a huge issue for Burt because of his judgment against his mother, and his criticism of Martha was especially hurtful because of her judgment against her father. We often find this type of interplay in marital counseling. Nevertheless, we must take care not to define the principle of sowing and reaping too narrowly, so that we develop deterministic teachings that have little or no support in Scripture. Having said that, I agree wholeheartedly that judgments against parents are often the root of marital problems, and for this insight I am indebted to the Sandfords. In spite of our differences in perspective, our "treatment" of Burt and Martha's problem would not be very different. Like the Sandfords, I would want to lead them in confession, repentance, rejection of the judgment they had made against their parents, and breaking its power in their lives and their marriage. After all, those steps – which Burt and Martha took as a result of the wise counsel of the Sandfords – brought restoration to their marriage! We do not need to accept fully the deterministic concept of "bitter-root judgments" to see that judgments against parents really are a "bitter root" that can undermine their Christian growth and their relationships with others.

Our survey reveals that there are various types of ungodly judgments that we can make as Christians. These judgments can vary as to their nature, their object, and their impact in a person's life. Nevertheless, if we are to avoid falling into the trap of judging God, ourselves, and others, we must press on to understand how ungodly judgments come about in the life of a believer. Only then can we be on our guard so that we do not allow ourselves to fall into sinful thoughts and attitudes.

Notes

1. On this topic, see the informative article by K.D. Lehman and C.E.T. Lehman, "Judgments and Bitterness Towards the Lord," 5 May 2006, <http://www.kclehman.com>.

2. In *The Divine Conspiracy* (London: Fount Paperbacks, 1998), Dallas Willard notes the connection between judging and condemning others. He correctly observes, "When we condemn another we really communicate that he or she is, in some deep and just possibly irredeemable way, bad – bad as a whole, and to be rejected" (240).

3. In many cases the damage inflicted on a child by his/her parents' words, and the judgments/expectations that he/she communicates, opens the way for Satan's work in the life of the child. Because of this, the parent's comments can function much in the same way as a curse, though they are not uttered as a curse in a technical sense.

4. On the possibility of demonic influence in the life of the believer, see Clinton E. Arnold, *3 Crucial Questions about Spiritual Warfare* (Grand Rapids, MI: Baker Books, 1997), 17–141.

5. Mario Bergner, *Setting Love in Order: Hope and Healing for the Homosexual* (Grand Rapids: Baker Books, 1995), 55.

6. *Ibid.*, 55–56.

7. Andy Comiskey's phrase "disavowal of the masculine" is accurate, but implies the presence of an underlying judgment; see *Pursuing Sexual Wholeness* (Lake Mary, FL: Charisma House, 1989), 114.

8. Experience shows that in certain extreme cases parents can be so abusive, even sadistic, in their relationship to their children that it is difficult to speak of positive characteristics. In such cases, we usually focus on forgiveness, repenting of the judgment, and healing from the impact of abuse. As healing occurs, we help the victim of abuse to establish new patterns in his relationship with his parents. He learns to love and honor them as far as possible while at the same time establishing proper boundaries in his relationship with them.

9. Sandford, *Restoring the Christian Family*, 196–211; *The Transformation of the Inner Man*, 237–266. More recently, see John and Mark Sandford, *A Comprehensive Guide to Deliverance and Inner Healing* (Grand Rapids: Chosen Books, 1992), 62–68.

10. Sandford, *Transformation of the Inner Man*, 237.

11. *Ibid.*, 238.

12. *Ibid.*, 239–240.

13. *Ibid.*, 242.

14. Paul cites the longer reiteration of this command from Deuteronomy 5:16.

15. *Ibid.*, 238–239.

16. I surveyed all the major commentaries on Matthew 7:1–2 and was unable to find even one writer who disagrees with this interpretation.

17. Sandford, *Transformation of the Inner Man*, 241.

18. *Ibid.*, 258.

19. *Ibid.*, 263.

20. This is especially true since, according to the Sandfords, a person's judgment inevitably draws to him people (especially a husband or wife) who tend to fulfill the judgment they have made. My disagreement with them is not that this is *possible* or even that it happens in some cases, but that it is *inevitable*. The word "inevitable" leads us beyond the teachings of Scripture.

Chapter 4

How Godly People Make Ungodly Judgments

───❦───

How do we fall into the trap of judging others? Often we find that the process is complex, involving a number of factors. In one case, a young man's mother was abusive to both her husband and her children, and finally left her husband for another man. The young man's father reacted by harboring great resentment against her and frequently waxed eloquent about women in the presence of his son. He told his son never to trust the opposite sex because "all women" are cunning and deceitful, and would break his heart if he gave them a chance. The father's words were hurtful to his son, but they seemed to make sense given his mother's betrayal of the entire family. At this point the seeds of a judgment were sown in the son's heart.

The impact of his father's words was not immediately evident in his life. During his later teen years, however, his feelings for several girls went unrequited, which left him feeling rejected and unloved. At that point the judgment against women, that had taken root as he reacted to the trauma of his mother's abandonment and accepted his father's harsh words, crystallized, and the impact of the judgment on his life became evident. He expected the worst of women and, for the most part, that is exactly what he experienced.

In the years following the crystallization of the judgment, the young man experienced great ambivalence in his relationships with the opposite sex. On the one hand, he was attracted to a number of women and desired to give his heart to them. On the other hand, however, he was fearful of being hurt and tended to maintain his distance emotionally from the women with whom he was involved. He always held back a portion of himself, which was dissatisfying both to him and to the women involved. After a while they separated, which was painful to him and thus strengthened the grip of the judgment on his life.

This young man's experience is similar to that of many believers who come to us for counseling. Often there are various factors that come together to bring them into bondage to the judgments that they have made. Nevertheless, it is helpful to consider these factors one by one in order to understand the way they work in our lives.

Factors that lead to ungodly judgments

There are basically four ways in which ungodly judgments come to be a part of a person's life. It is important for us to understand these processes so we can be on our guard against judgments in our own lives and use them to discover when ungodly judgments are the root issues in the life of another person.

Inheritance

The first way in which we come to judge others is through *inheritance*. In many cases, for example, a mother's strong judgment against men, especially in the context of marriage, will open the way for evil spirits to work, not only in her life, but also in the lives of her children. The consequence of the mother's judgment, namely the influence of demonic powers, is passed down naturally to the child. These deceiving spirits can influence the perceptions of the child toward certain individuals or groups, so that almost without realizing what is happening she herself slips into ungodly judgments. She may assume that any man who marries her will abuse her or leave her, or she may assume that all he wants is sex. As a result some people delay marriage, or they may enter marriage with a host of negative expectations that can become self-fulfilling prophecies. When we lead people in repenting of the judgment they have made and challenge any spirits that were passed down to them as a result of their mother's judgment, we frequently witness demonic manifestations leading to a strong and decisive deliverance from the spirit's power. Of course, a father's strong judgment against women could also be passed down to his children, but I have focused here on a mother's judgment against men since in my experience this type of generational transmission is more common.

I recognize that this teaching is controversial and affirm that there is no single verse that teaches directly that parental sin or occult involvement can result in demonic influence in the lives of subsequent generations. Verses about the sins of the fathers being visited on descendants up to the third and fourth generations (e.g. Exodus 20:5; Deuteronomy 5:9), which are often cited in support of this teaching by deliverance practitioners, refer to the punishment for sin under the Mosaic Covenant, not demonic influence. This data, on its own, is insufficient to support the belief that the consequences of a parent's judgment can fall on his or her child.

So why do I suggest inheritance as one of the ways judgments can come into the life of a believer? Four lines of evidence lead me to this conclusion. First, at least one deliverance account in the gospels points to demonization resulting from inheritance as a distinct possibility. In Mark 9:21 the father of a demonized boy affirms that his son had been tormented by the spirit "from childhood." The simplest explanation of how the boy came to be in that condition is that a spirit was passed down to him.[1]

Second, most of us affirm that the consequences of a parent's sin often impact his or her children. For example, a mother who has contracted AIDS through extramarital sex can pass the virus on to her baby, or a father who gambles compulsively can lead his children into poverty. If that is the case, why is it so hard to believe that demonic influence resulting from a parent's sin can be passed down to his or her child? Would not a spirit press its advantage in the situation as far as possible?

Third, we often observe that children demonstrate some of the same sinful patterns of behavior as their parents. "He has his daddy's temper," we might say. This tendency is documented in Scripture, as when the kings of Israel engage in the same sinful practices that were committed by their parents (e.g. 1 Kings 15:3). We usually assume that the cycle is repeated because of parental teaching and example, or because of genetic inheritance, and these are certainly important factors, but can we rule out the possibility that demonic influence is involved as well? If so, on what basis can we reject this possibility?

Fourth, over the many years that I have been involved in counseling, inner healing, and deliverance ministries, I have participated in the following pattern of ministry hundreds of times. We recognize the possibility that demonic influence has been inherited due to a correlation of the parent's sin, occult involvement, and lifestyle with the problems experienced by the counselee. On that basis we challenge gently but firmly any spirits that have been passed down to the counselee from his parent. In many cases this results in a bit of a struggle (or in some cases a dramatic struggle!), and the person experiences sudden and unusual physical symptoms. After a short time, these symptoms disappear and it seems the deliverance is over. The next week the person reports a significant reduction in symptoms such as fear, lustful urges, accusing thoughts, or difficulties in prayer.[2] I have personally witnessed this pattern in hundreds of ministry sessions with believers. Is not the simplest and most probable explanation for the repetitive nature of this pattern and its success in the lives of so many people simply this – that demonic influence really can pass down from one generation to another?

I recognize that the evidence I have set forth in this section may be unconvincing to some readers. Why is that? For one thing, the case for the teaching that demonic influence can come into the life of a child through the sin of his or her parent is far from airtight. Scripture certainly does not contradict this teaching, but then again neither does the Bible set forth directly a doctrine of demonic inheritance. For another thing, many Christians regard the phenomenon of demonic influence itself as something that occurs only rarely and then in extreme cases. Of course, this assumption is far from what we see in the teaching and ministry of Jesus and His followers (see, for example, Matthew 8:16–17; Mark 1:32–34; 1:39; 3:10–12; Luke 4:40–41; 13:32), but it seems to fit with their experience. Having attended church for years without having witnessed a demonic manifestation, they tend to adopt biological or psychological explanations for people's problems and dismiss the possibility of a demonic component.

That is where I was ten years ago. Lacking the understanding to recognize the possibility of demonic influence in the lives of counselees, I never challenged a spirit and commanded it to leave. For that reason, I never witnessed the reality of spiritual conflict first hand. Yet something in me remained uneasy, especially when I read in the gospels and Acts that deliverance was a regular and vital part of Jesus' ministry and the ministry of His disciples. I longed to help people experience radical change, just as Jesus did, but it was not until I stepped out in faith and challenged evil spirits in the lives of certain counselees that I saw the reality of the spirit world first hand. My ministry was literally transformed.

If the reader is open to the possibility of demonic influence by inheritance, it is important that he or she be able to recognize when this factor has played a significant role in the development of a judgment. Making this determination requires that we understand both the symptoms that the person is experiencing and their family background to see if we can make a correlation between the two. For example, perhaps a counselee comes to us because she is cold and distant in her relationships with men, in which case we need to ask about her family background. If we find, for example, that the counselee's mother was abused by her father and one of her brothers and seems to have made a judgment against men based on these negative experiences, then we need to consider the possibility that her daughter's similar problems are related. Of course, the daughter could have made a judgment on men early in life as a result of exposure to the bitter way her mother related to men and spoke of them, but it is possible that inheritance played an important role as well. Experience has shown that this is often the case. Ultimately, however, we can only know for sure by challenging any spirits that may have been transferred down to her from her mother and observing what happens. If an inherited spirit is present, we can usually tell by (1) the struggle or manifestation that takes place, (2) by the sense of release that the counselee reports after the deliverance, and/or (3) the reduction in symptoms that is experienced after the deliverance.

Parental teachings and example

The second way in which we come to judge others is through *parental teachings and example*. I am listing this factor independently because of the huge impact it has in a person's life. Of course, the teachings and example of a parent can reinforce the work of deceiving spirits that are passed down through inheritance, but such teachings and examples can also work on their own to lead someone into making ungodly judgments. In practice, the only way to distinguish between the two influences in the life of a counselee is to challenge any spirits that have been passed down from his mother or father and see what happens. If the person begins to experience symptoms that are often associated with deliverance and then reports a sense of release, we usually conclude that a spirit had indeed passed down the family line to them. This does not mean, however, that the parents' judgmental teachings and example have not also influenced the counselee's thinking and feelings toward a certain person or group of people.

The most common example of this kind of judgment is prejudice against certain races and people groups. When a child witnesses his parents' hatred for a particular group and listens to their negative comments about them, it is natural for him to internalize his parent's negative feelings and perspective toward that particular group. From that point on he will view people from that group through the lens of his parents' prejudice, which will both limit and color any interactions that occur with them. In the end, the initial judgment is reinforced and strengthened time and time again until an impenetrable wall exists between the child and the people that he has judged.

How can we discern when judgments have originated from parental teachings or example? We should explore this possibility by listening carefully to the counselee as he discusses his parents' attitudes toward the person or group in question. We should ask how his parents spoke about the person or group, whether they related to them at all, and, if they did, how they interacted with them. Then we should ask the counselee how he felt when he heard his parents' negative comments and saw their lack of regard for this person or group. In this way we should be able to find out if the counselee feels that he was influenced substantially by his parents' teachings and example. Of course, his answers may reflect a certain subjectivity, and he may feel that he was not influenced by his parents when in fact the impact of their teachings and example was significant. If we suspect that this may indeed be the case, we can eliminate other possibilities, then gently suggest the possibility to him and observe his reaction. Or we can go to the Lord in prayer, asking Him to reveal the roots of the counselee's judgment, and see what happens. In certain cases the Spirit has revealed the source of the problem in a way that the counselee can accept even if he is fairly closed to input from others, including his counselor.

The ungodly counsel of others

The third way in which we come to judge others is through *the ungodly counsel of others* outside our families. Such counsel can be especially influential especially during the teen years when peers typically become all-important in a person's life. A teen's negative experience with a person or a class of people can become the basis for a judgment on that person or group. Due to her influence on other teens, her negative comments can become the basis for them to make a similar judgment on the same person or group. Certain teens are judged as "dorky" or "uncool," and thus unworthy of friendship, due to the shared perceptions of a number of friends.

Another example might be helpful as well. A teen's judgment on certain authority figures can become the basis for her friend's judgment on authority figures in general and her rebellion against them. In such cases, judgments are made against others not because of negative experiences with the person or group, but due to the negative comments of others. Once the judgment is in place, it will typically color the person's interpretation of the authority figure, further strengthening the judgment's power in their life and causing them to view her or him in an increasingly negative light. Of course, such influence is not confined to the teenage years. Many adults also fall into the same types of ungodly judgments based not on first-hand experience, but on the judgmental comments of others.

In counseling we should look first to other potential sources of a judgment that are closer to the person such as inheritance and parental teachings and example. The reason is that most judgments originate there. If, however, we do not find the source of the judgment within the family, then we are justified in extending our search to other sources of input. Ultimately, we must seek the answer to the question, "Who influenced you to make this judgment against the other person or group?" Once we have found the answer to that question, we will understand the specific circumstances surrounding the judgment. At that point we will be in a position to help the counselee to repent of it and break its influence in his life.

Our ungodly responses to trauma

The fourth way in which we come to judge others is through *our ungodly responses to various kinds of trauma.* I am using the word "trauma" here in a broad sense to include both (1) traumatic experiences that are out of human control such as natural disasters, a major illness, the sudden death of a loved one, or a financial reversal, and (2) traumatic experiences that result from human sinfulness. This latter type of trauma includes others' words and actions that deeply wound a person's heart, emotional, physical or sexual abuse, betrayal by a loved one, divorce, and all kinds of violent behavior.

When believers experience trauma and hardships of any kind, it is an opportunity for them to grow closer to the "God of all comfort" (2 Corinthians 1:3). It is also, however, an opportunity that the enemy can use to his own advantage, especially through deception. Often we are deceived due to (1) our own false or incomplete interpretations of the trauma we have endured, (2) others' interpretations of those events, (3) thoughts that are suggested by deceiving spirits, or, as is most common, (4) a combination of these factors. These false ideas and interpretations can influence our views of ourselves and others. If these false notions are not rejected, but instead are embraced as true, the person involved often slips into an ungodly judgment, often without knowing it.[3]

Many examples can be given of this process that leads us into ungodly judgments. Often people react to trauma by making judgments against God. They may become angry with God after the death of a loved one, label Him as "evil," "capricious," or "uncaring," and turn their back on the One who longs to bring comfort and healing in the midst of their trauma. Or they may become disappointed with God due to prayers that appear to be unanswered and give up bringing their concerns to Him. The enemy loves to use our judgments against God to separate us from the source of our life and strength.

It is also common for people to respond to trauma by making deep judgments against themselves. They may judge themselves as "guilty" or "unworthy" because they blame themselves for their parents' divorce. A child who is treated badly by his parents often judges himself as deserving of such treatment. Or a victim of rape or sexual abuse may judge herself as "damaged," "dirty" or undeserving of the love of a decent, loving husband. Often she *feels* that somehow the rape or abuse was her fault, though intellectually she *believes* that she was an unwilling victim and that the abuser was the one who sinned against her. In such cases the deception is usually buried deep within her heart. Renouncing the judgment is helpful in that the person chooses to embrace the truth that brings freedom and to reject the deception that is holding her in bondage. Often, however, such renunciations will not, in themselves, set the victim free from the feelings of guilt and shame that have haunted her since she was abused. They must be followed by healing prayer, in which we ask the Holy Spirit to take away the false guilt and shame, and to reveal God's love and truth in her inner being. With the Apostle Paul, we pray that she, "being rooted and established in love, may have power, together with all the saints, to grasp how wide and long and high and deep is the love of Christ, and to know this love that surpasses knowledge" (Ephesians 3:17b–19a).[4] Then we wait quietly to see what the Lord will do. Often the results of this type of prayer are dramatic.

Finally, people can react to trauma by judging other people. For example, a person who is wounded and betrayed by another may determine that people in general are untrustworthy and will hurt you if given the chance. Once this determination (judgment) is made, then the person may fall into a number of types of ungodly responses in order to protect themselves from harm. They may close their heart to others or build emotional walls to keep others at a safe distance. Or they may become aggressive and critical in their interactions with others, believing that the best defense against hurt is a good offense. Of course, this kind of strategy may eliminate some hurt, but it also precludes the possibility of intimacy with others and meaningful fellowship with other members of the body of Christ. Ultimately, they would be much better off bringing their trauma to the Lord for healing, releasing their fears into His hands, and trusting Him to be their Shield and Protector. Then they can develop the wisdom they need to discern the character of others and to determine who is worthy of their trust and who is not.

In some cases these various deceptions that underlie these types of judgments are embraced primarily at an intellectual level, in which case the person must renounce them decisively and choose to embrace the truth of God's Word. Such a commitment on the counselee's part is essential if he is to walk in freedom and victory in Christ. In other cases, however, the deception is deeply rooted and functions more at a heart-level. The person may believe one thing with their mind, yet feel something quite different in their heart, and it is often the heart-level conviction that has the greater impact on their feelings, behavior, and relationships with others. While specific renunciations of the lies are important in many cases, healing prayer is also needed in which the Lord intervenes to eliminate the power of the deceptions and to apply His truth to the deepest places of our hearts. Only then can we be free from deception and break the power of the judgment in our lives and relationships.

Once again, the process of developing judgments is often complex, involving more than one of these influences. It often begins early in life as we are exposed to ungodly influences and traumatic experiences. And if we analyze the process by which judgments develop, we observe that it frequently involves a number of stages, each of which will typically become distinct and recognizable as we move through the counseling process.

The process of developing ungodly judgments

As I have listened to the life-stories of hundreds of counselees, I have observed that the process of developing judgments, especially generalizing judgments against certain groups of people, typically unfolds in three stages. I like to call these three stages "seed-sowing," "crystallization," and "snowballing."

Seed-sowing

Seeds of a judgment can be sown in a child's life in the various ways that were mentioned above. In specific terms, what does that involve? In the case of judgments that are sown through inheritance, if a child's mother's or father's life is being controlled by a judgment against certain people or groups, especially at the time the child is conceived or is growing in his mother's womb, the seeds of a judgment can be passed down to the child. Deceiving spirits that have been working in the parent's life can transfer to the child and stimulate negative thoughts and feelings toward the group in question.

When I have prayed and asked the Holy Spirit to reveal the origins of controlling judgments, in certain cases it has become clear to the counselee, and also to me, that the effects of the judgment were present from the very beginning of their lives.[5] For example, one counselee had a controlling judgment against men, which seemed to originate in the life of her mother, who had been violently raped by more than one man. As we prayed, she sensed the Holy Spirit revealing to her that this judgment had not originated from an experience in her life, but had been transmitted directly to her from her mother. When she renounced the judgment and chose to accept men as God's creation, we commanded any spirits who were working in connection with the judgment to leave. At that point she experienced a strong and decisive deliverance, and since then has enjoyed a new freedom in her relationships with men, including her husband.

The process is a little different in cases in which a judgment is sown through the teaching and example of the parents. We must keep in mind that children are incredibly teachable and will often internalize the beliefs and values of their parents long before they are able to evaluate them critically and rationally. We should give thanks for this characteristic because it enables godly parents to pass on their faith and values to their children with relative ease. Nevertheless, a child's teachability also means that he will tend to embrace not only the positive beliefs and values of his parents, but their negative attitudes and judgments as well.

When parents avoid or badmouth a certain group of people, the judgment that they are expressing in this way tends to be picked up by their children. As the children grow, they, too, often begin to voice their displeasure and distrust toward the group in question, so that the judgment permeates the entire household. After a while the family avoids people from that group, or if they do relate to them, the relationships are characterized by a strong sense of ambivalence. A relatively high percentage of children who are raised in such an environment embrace at least to some degree their parents' judgment and, in turn, pass it on to their children.

When judgments are sown through a person's ungodly or unhealthy responses to trauma, the process is a little different.

We have already discussed the ways in which judgments toward God, toward ourselves and toward others can grow out of our reactions to traumatic events that seem to threaten our security and existence as a child, such as the divorce of our parents. Though these events often occur when children are very young, their reactions can stick with them a long time, even into adulthood.

The seeds that are sown in a person's life either by inheritance, a parent's teaching and example, and their ungodly or unhealthy responses to trauma provide the core around which a judgment can grow and develop. Nevertheless, in many cases the impact of the judgment is still hidden. Only later, when the judgment crystallizes, will we be able to observe its effects in their life.

Crystallization

In many cases we have observed a specific point in a person's life when a controlling judgment takes shape, or crystallizes. Beginning at that point, which often occurs in conjunction with a traumatic event, the power of the judgment becomes increasingly evident in their life.

At times the judgment crystallizes in relation to another individual. I recall, for example, a pastor's daughter who came to me for counseling. Her father was a harsh, controlling individual, who had a broad perfectionist streak. No matter how hard his daughter tried, she could never please him. He criticized her frequently and hardly ever praised her for her efforts. As a result, she grew up without experiencing a father's love and approval.

When I asked about her teen years, which were characterized by tremendous rebellion, she mentioned one experience that stood out in her memory. One day she had given her best effort to help her father in hopes of pleasing him, and he responded with criticism that was particularly scathing. She remembers vividly her reaction to his words and demeanor. In her heart she said, "Watch out!" At that point, as she explained it, she closed her heart to her father and judged him harshly. She then set out on a course of rebellion that was both a search for love and a determined effort to exact revenge against her father. The results were tragic, both for the daughter and for the entire family.

In other cases the judgment crystallizes in relation to a group of people. One young woman who came to me for counseling shared her sad story of abuse. During her childhood she was sexually abused by her older brothers, but that only sowed the seeds of a judgment against men. The critical point of crystallization came several years later when, while she was still a pre-teen, her own father attempted to molest her. At that point the judgment against men took shape and began to influence all of her relationships with the opposite sex.

When a judgment crystallizes in this way, often during the pre-teen or teen years, it is often accompanied by an inner vow: "I'll show him!" "I'll never let another man hurt me." "I'll never be friends with another person like her." Where there is a judgment, there is usually a vow, and vice versa. Often, however, a person's difficulties increase dramatically after the judgment crystallizes and they take an inner vow. In the ministry of deliverance, we find that judgments and vows frequently give the Enemy an opportunity to work in a person's life. Only when they are willing to repent of the judgments and the vows that they have made, and break their power in their lives, are they set free to know the blessing and victory that God desires for them.

Snowballing
After the judgment crystallizes and its power is evident in a person's life, they often move into the stage that I like to call "snowballing." Having judged another person or a certain group of people, they expect them to act in accordance with their judgment. In short, they expect the worst of them, and in

their own strength, using all of their fleshly defenses, they attempt to stop the inevitable. In spite of their efforts, however, their subsequent experiences with the person or group in question are typically negative. These difficult and unpleasant experiences reinforce the initial judgment, which further strengthens its impact on the person's life.

As I mentioned earlier, I do not believe this process is merely psychological in nature, though the negative expectations we have in relation to those we have judged certainly play an important part. Doubtless, in many cases, they become self-fulfilling prophecies. Also, low self-image frequently plays a critical role. When we feel unworthy of being treated with dignity and respect, we may signal to others, often in subtle ways, that we are ready to receive abuse. In a sense, our own deception and self-judgments serve to validate their victimization. Nevertheless, I have no doubt that the Enemy is also involved, having been given an opportunity to work in our lives through the judgment and the vows that we have made.[6] For these reasons many women who have been treated badly by their father, their brothers, or other men in their lives often seem to draw to themselves boyfriends and husbands who treat them badly. It seems that the Enemy has marked them as a victim, so that abusive men – victimizers, in fact – are drawn to them. It is almost as if they have a flashing sign on their forehead that says, "Abuse me!" The horrible things they experience at the hands of abusive men frequently tighten the grip of the judgment on their lives and their relationships.[7]

The analogy of a snowball is appropriate as we seek to describe this process. As a judgment crystallizes, it functions very much like a magnet, drawing to itself other negative experiences that reinforce its power in a person's life. Like a snowball that begins to roll down a hill, it gradually increases in size until eventually it can reach massive proportions. What began as a tiny seed of a judgment then crystallized as a result of subsequent experiences that were painful or humiliating, and eventually became a controlling force for evil in their life. Only the power and love of Christ can set the person free from bondage and lead them into the glorious freedom that God desires for them as His children.

Notes

1. See Clinton E. Arnold, *3 Crucial Questions about Spiritual Warfare* (Grand Rapids, MI: Baker Books, 1997), 113, 119.

2. This occurs particularly in cases of *primary demonization*, where the particular symptoms that the person is experiencing are present primarily because of the presence and work of an evil spirit, often due to inheritance or the person's involvement in occult-related activities. In this type of situation, deliverance is a highly effective treatment, often yielding dramatic and immediate results very much like the deliverance ministry of Jesus. We should distinguish between this phenomenon and *secondary demonization*, where demonic influence is secondary to emotional woundedness, deep-level deception, and unhealthy/ungodly responses to traumatic experiences in a person's life. In such cases, evil spirits "piggyback" onto existing problems, on the one hand defending the strongholds that have been established in a person's life and, on the other hand, working to exacerbate the impact of the emotional/sin issues that are already present. In cases of secondary demonization, deliverance without inner healing/forgiveness/repentance usually produces only limited and temporary results. In conjunction with these other ministries, however, deliverance is an effective tool that provides additional relief from the presenting symptoms of many problems.

3. The importance of deeply-rooted lies as the basis for people's pain in the present is the fundamental principle underlying Theophostic Ministry; see Edward M. Smith, *Healing Life's Hurts through Theophostic Prayer* (Ventura, CA: Regal Books, 2002), as well as the more detailed training materials written by Smith that are put out by Theophostic Prayer Ministries. By stressing the importance of deception in the formation of judgments, I do not mean to imply that people are merely passive in this whole process. In this I agree with Maier and Monroe in their criticism of the theological basis for Theophostic Ministry; see Bryan N. Maier and Philip G. Monroe, "A Theological Analysis of Theophostic Ministry," *Trinity Journal* 24NS (2003), 176–178, though this criticism relates more to Smith's interpretation of the Theophostic process than to the ministry process itself. Human beings are ultimately ripe for deception due to our inherent sinful tendency toward self-deception.

Still, Maier and Monroe fail to mention that deception can also take root in our hearts during childhood due to where we are in the developmental process.

4. A focused approach that is useful in this type of situation is Theophostic Ministry, though in my experience the same dramatic results are often achieved through healing prayer of a more general nature. In both cases, the Lord reveals His truth in the person's heart, effectively neutralizing the deception that has been holding them in bondage. Unfortunately, however, the Theophostic methodology is so specific and focused that the training materials give the impression, at least to some, of discounting the effectiveness of normal spiritual disciplines such as "reading and memorizing God's word, reading Christian authors, praying, meditating on God's character and actions, listening to preaching and teaching, engaging in self-examination, etc." (Maier and Monroe, 186), though in his 2005 revision of the *Theophostic Prayer Ministry Basic Seminar Manual*, Smith explicitly denies that he minimizes the importance of these disciplines (see chapter 1). Similarly, I do not mean in any way to discount the power of these disciplines in the life of a believer. Rather, I view all these disciplines as vital to Christian growth, but also emphasize the need for specific prayer for the Spirit's work to deepen our understanding of God's word and to apply it to our hearts, so that the word of Christ dwells in us richly. Such prayer is often needed so that we can be set free of the deep-level deceptions that hold us in bondage.

5. When we are unsure as to the origin of a particular judgment, we often go to the Lord in prayer, asking that He would reveal to us the roots of the problem. Then we wait quietly for His leading, which may come to the counselee or to a member of the ministry team. God has been consistently faithful to provide the insights that we need to lead the counselee forward in repentance and healing, provided we are patient and wait for His direction.

6. As in many aspects of ministry, we must maintain a balance here, just as we must maintain a balance between acknowledging the influence of the world, the flesh, and the devil. Many deliverance ministries fail at this point, and focus all of their attention on one aspect of the problem; cf. Arnold, *3 Crucial Questions*, 32–37.

7. This principle is observed by John Eldredge in his book, *Waking the Dead* (Nashville: Thomas Nelson Publishers, 2003), "There is a gravitational field the Enemy creates around a person that pulls everyone in her life to do to her what he is doing to her" (170).

Chapter 5

THE IMPACT OF
UNGODLY JUDGMENTS

What's so bad about making judgments against others, especially others who hurt or offend us? After all, don't they deserve it? As one counselee blurted out, "Why shouldn't I hate them and judge them? Let me tell you what they did to me!" As she told me her story, I found myself sympathizing with her. The rejection and abuse that she had endured at the hands of family members was horrific. I could certainly understand her abhorrence of them. Yet I knew what she needed to do. After taking some time to listen, to empathize with her and to validate her feelings, I explained that there was only one road to freedom and victory. As difficult as it would undoubtedly be, she must forgive them for the things they did to her and repent of the judgment she had made in her heart against them. I shared with her that this does not mean that she should deny her hurt or pretend that the abuse never happened. Rather she must acknowledge the hurt, release it to God, and choose the way of obedience. Just as she received God's grace in Christ, she must also become a channel of His grace to others, beginning with the family members who abused her. And judgments are incompatible with the principle of grace.

"Why shouldn't I hate them and judge them?" We have all asked that question at one time or another when we have experienced mistreatment and abuse. In many cases such a response is certainly understandable given the magnitude of the abuse and injustice that we have experienced. However, the reality is that ungodly judgments, like other forms of sin, typically bring undesirable consequences into our lives. We are the ones who suffer as a result of the judgments we have made. In this chapter we are going to explore some of the ways in which we suffer as we discuss specific consequences of making ungodly judgments against God, ourselves, and others.

We experience some distance in our relationship with God

As we have observed earlier in this study, when we judge others, we violate several principles that are foundational in the New Testament. We seem oblivious to the fact that God did not judge us in spite of our sin, but rather forgave us and accepted us completely in Christ. We reject the attitude of humility that Jesus modeled and taught to His disciples, and adopt a superior position in relation to our brothers and sisters in Christ. And, finally, we take to ourselves something that rightfully belongs to God alone, that is, the right to judge humanity. The result, according to the Apostle Paul, is that we "judge someone else's servant" (Romans 14:4).

When we judge another person, we sin against God. As with other forms of sin, making and maintaining ungodly judgments often brings a sense of distance from God. It's not that He rejects us or turns His back on us; it's just that something isn't right between us. We struggle in prayer. We lack the faith to come to God boldly, confident that He will hear and answer our requests. We are tentative and hesitant in our relationship to the Father, knowing deep within that the judgments we have made against others are bringing grief to His heart. We are, of course, still His children simply because of our faith in Christ, but as a result of the judgments we have made against others for whom Christ died, we are unable to enjoy the fullness of our relationship with Him. Many Christians are in this position, and often they do not realize it.

Though all judgments can cause us to experience distance in our relationship with our heavenly Father, one type of judgment is especially dangerous in this regard. When we judge God Himself because we are dissatisfied with our life or do not understand why we have experienced various difficulties or traumas, we inevitably experience a coldness in our relationship with Him. In some cases the judgment is long forgotten, yet the coldness and distance remain until the person repents of the judgment and breaks its power.

Some years ago I became acquainted with a woman whose life was tragic. Before I met this woman, her daughter, to whom she was very close, died after a lengthy illness. Not long afterwards her husband also passed away. While her situation was tragic, her reaction to her loss was even more so. She harbored terrible bitterness against God and judged Him in her heart. I remember sitting next to her at church one morning years after the loss of her daughter and her husband. In the moments just before the service began, when most people were chatting quietly or preparing their heart for worship, she suddenly turned to me with an angry look on her face. "Why did God take my daughter and husband?" she blurted out. "I thought He loved me!" How could this woman, whose heart was full of bitterness and a deep judgment against God, possibly draw close to the Father in worship and adoration?

I do not mean to imply that as believers we never experience disappointment or even anger in our relationship to God. If we are honest, we all struggle at times with these feelings. Many people, however, do not know how to handle their feelings in a manner that leads to resolution and renewal in their relationship with the Lord. Some Christians deny their feelings, unable to face the fact that they are disappointed or angry with God, while others nurse their feelings, which over time harden into bitterness and a judgmental attitude toward the Lord. In contrast to these approaches, I believe that honesty and openness in our relationship with God is the first step toward healing and wholeness. We need to learn to cry out to the Lord as David does in the Psalms,

> Why, O LORD, do you stand far off?
>   Why do you hide yourself in times of trouble?
>
> (10:1)

David was not afraid to bring his hard questions to the Lord, and we must have the courage to do the same.[1] Yet David's heart remained open to the Lord, and ultimately he always came back to a position of faith:

> But you, O God, do see trouble and grief;
>   you consider it to take it in hand.
>
> (10:14)

How does David do that? Though he expresses his disappointment and anger honestly, he does not close his heart against the Lord or make a judgment against Him. As a result, God reveals more of Himself to him. He may never know the answer to the question, "Why...?", but he does know God more and more intimately. He is a man after God's own heart.

The Evil One loves it when we judge God, because this type of judgment cuts us off from the Source of our life and strength. In fact, evil spirits often suggest judgmental thoughts against God, especially following traumatic experiences, in hopes that we will receive them and make them our own. From these seeds often grow deeply-rooted judgments that come between us and the One who loves us with a perfect and an everlasting love. In this way we are neutralized in spiritual conflict and do not bear fruit for God's glory in our lives and ministries.

We limit ourselves and God's work in our lives

Often people who have made judgments against others impose various limitations on themselves, and in so doing they limit the scope of their experiences and the ways in which God can work in their lives. For example, some years ago I took part in a prayer and counseling ministry with a young seminary graduate. This young lady had two strikes against her from the start. For one thing, she came from a family where the members rarely spoke kindly to one another and almost never encouraged each other. Instead, they wounded each other almost constantly. As if this was not enough, there was also a strong spirit of fear that had come down her mother's line, whose work was evident in all of the children in the family. We know this because she, her mother, and all her siblings were exceedingly fearful, and when we gently challenged this spirit she began manifesting quite strongly before the spirit left her. In subsequent sessions she reported a marked reduction in fear.

The result of these two influences was that she was afraid others would hurt her if she opened her heart to them. She judged all human beings as being "untrustworthy," and on that basis she distanced herself from them. She hardened her heart and built an invisible wall around herself to keep others at a safe distance. From that position of safety, she related to others as potential enemies. She was hard and demanding in her demeanor. Needless to say, other people tended to react negatively to her relational style.

Thankfully, this young lady realized her need to be set free from the negative patterns she had developed, and the Lord worked powerfully to release her from bondage. This involved confessing the fact that she had erected walls to protect herself rather than allowing God to be her Protector. She also rejected and released the judgment she had made against others and made the decision to risk opening up her heart to them. She expressed her repentance and her new commitment to God in prayer, and then took the step of attempting to form new habits of relating to others. Of course, this decision wasn't easy for her, but it brought tremendous freedom into her life and influenced positively both the number and depth of her relationships.[2] As she progressed in counseling, she realized just how much the judgment she made against others had limited the depth of her relationships with others, and consequently God's sanctifying work in her life.

Not everyone's judgment is as broad and far-reaching as this young lady's, but judgments often limit our relationships with certain groups of people. Many people who have been hurt deeply by a member of a particular group tend to judge all members of that group as untrustworthy, and as a result they keep their distance so as not to be hurt. Of course, when we make such judgments we are really embracing a deception, since it is both untrue and unfair to lump all members of a group together and brand them as untrustworthy. In the end, however, we are the ones that are hurt by the judgments we make, regardless of whether we judge others based on gender, age, race, occupation, social position, or other factors.

Several days ago a young woman who is in Christian service asked me to pray for her. She hopes to marry and to have a family, but she has had trouble in her relationships with men. In the past when a relationship was developing with a man that she found attractive, she has been driven by something she does not understand to pull back and break off the relationship. As we prayed and asked the Lord's direction, we discovered a strong judgment against her father, who had treated her very badly. Apparently this judgment had generalized and was causing her to pull back from men who could become a good husband to her. Deep in her heart she expected them to be unfaithful, just as her father had been unfaithful to her and her mother. Though God was working to provide a godly husband for her, the judgment in her heart was leading her to reject His provision for her.

It is simply a fact of life that judgments limit us. They limit the depth of relationship that we enjoy with other people and with specific groups of people. They also limit the ministries that we can have with certain types of people. And since God often blesses and teaches us through our relationships with others, they limit God's gracious work in our lives.

We hinder God's work in another person's life

This consequence is especially sobering. When we judge other people, we telegraph these judgments to them in various ways. Sometimes we declare our judgment outright, while at other times our judgment becomes the implicit basis for the way in which we relate to them. In either case, sooner or later the person usually realizes the nature of the judgment we have made against them.

Once the person becomes aware that we have judged them, our judgment may wound them deeply, leading to a response of anger and bitterness that may be used to open the way for Satan's ungodly influence in their life. Our judgment may also lodge deeply within their heart, thus damaging the person's self-image. As a result, they may find it difficult to step out in faith, believing that God will use them in wonderful ways and glorify Himself through their life. Instead, they approach life and ministry with a negative expectation resulting from the internalization of our judgment against them. God may use others, but He definitely will not use them. Or so they think. Our judgment can actually oppose and limit God's gracious work in their life.

It is amazing to see the power that judgments can have in a

person's life, especially when they are pronounced early in life or are made by parents or other authority figures. In fact, many writers in the area of inner healing refer to such negative pronouncements as "curses" since they can be used by demonic forces to influence powerfully a person's life.[3] I do not know how many people I have met whose performance in school was sub-standard due to the fact that a parent or other authority figure pronounced them "dumb" or "stupid." Others struggle in many areas of life due to the judgment that "they'd never amount to anything." And in some cases, people receive judgments that relate to their fundamental character. Some are labeled "no good," "evil," or "worthless."

These kinds of judgments can lead a person to view themselves in a highly subjective manner. One young Asian woman who came for counseling had been labeled because of her appearance. Though she was a lovely woman, all the family members agreed that her older sisters were lovelier still, and they taunted her mercilessly. When they would gather together for family events, it was not uncommon for them to sing a taunting song about how she was "dark," "flat-faced," and "ugly." Not surprisingly, this young woman received the judgment as true – after all, it came from her own family – and judged herself as unattractive. Interestingly enough, when we asked God to reveal His truth to her in response to this judgment, He answered our prayer in an unexpected way. He reminded her of the fact that she had participated twice in local beauty contests, in one case winning the contest and in the other case coming in as a runner-up!

These are only a few examples. Actually, there are many types of careless judgments we make against others that can limit their options and oppose the work of God in them and through them. And it is no small thing to oppose the work of God in the life of another person who is created in the image of God, especially when it is a fellow believer for whom Christ died!

We give the devil an opportunity to work in our lives and our relationships

On what basis can I say that our judgments give the Evil One an opportunity to work in our lives? Most important here is the relationship between forgiving the sins of others and repenting of the judgments that we have made against them.[4] The fact of the matter is that we cannot say we have truly forgiven someone until we have repented of the judgments we have made against them in our hearts. Thus, repenting of judgments we have made is an important component of forgiveness.

We must consider in a new way the implications of Ephesians 4:26–27,

> "In your anger do not sin": Do not let the sun go down while you are still angry, and do not give the devil a foothold.

Since unforgiveness gives the devil an opportunity to work in our lives and our relationships with others, we should not be surprised to find that making judgments against others can also do much the same thing.

The truth of this scriptural principle is frequently confirmed in our counseling sessions. When the person we are counseling repents of a judgment they have made against another, or rejects a judgment that was made against them, we often use our spiritual authority in Christ to break the power of the judgment in their life. Then we usually challenge gently any evil spirits that have been given an opportunity to work in the person's life as a result of that judgment, commanding them to leave and not return.

Many times we have seen evidence of demonic resistance at that point. For example, the individual may suddenly become dizzy, confused, or sleepy. They may also experience strange sensations or discomfort in some part of their body, or in some cases experience a fit of coughing or dry heaves as the spirit is expelled. As we focus our commands on the demon that is causing these sensations, it yields to our authority in Christ, and the sensations disappear. What is important to note, however, is the fact that our judgments against others can give the enemy an opportunity to work in us. And, of course, these evil spirits are reluctant to give up the ground that they have held in our lives for some time.

We open the door for judgments to come back on us

I mention this consequence as a result of our team's experience in life and ministry. In our experience, if we make ungodly judgments against others, these same people often make judgments against us.[5] This appears to be consistent with the teaching of Luke 6:37–38:

> Do not judge, and you will not be judged. Do not condemn, and you will not be condemned. Forgive, and you will be forgiven. Give, and it will be given to you. A good measure, pressed down, shaken together and running over, will be poured into your lap. For with the measure you use, it will be measured to you.

Thus there seems to be a spiritual principle involved in certain cases, apart from the fact that people often react negatively to us in response to the judgments that we are telegraphing to them, whether consciously or unconsciously.[6]

I myself experienced this consequence firsthand. Several years ago I was appointed to a leadership position in a Christian organization. As I began exercising leadership and making some needed changes in the organization, a few of the leaders serving below me in the organizational structure began reacting very negatively to my leadership. In fact, you could say that they almost went crazy with resentment and anger. I knew that I was making changes in areas in which they had traditionally wielded authority, but I must admit I was puzzled at the extreme nature of their reaction. The fact is I have never seen anyone respond to my leadership in that way.

As I was expressing my confusion to God in prayer, the Lord convicted me of the fact that I had judged these particular leaders long before they had judged me. He also suggested that this was the reason for their extreme reaction. At that point I repented of my judgment against them and took the initiative in listening sympathetically to their complaints, after which the situation improved dramatically. I'm sure my willingness to listen helped a lot, but I am also convinced that the dramatic change that occurred cannot be explained simply on that basis. I believe my willingness to repent of and release the judgment I had made against them previously had a lot to do with the change that occurred in the relationship, though I did not mention the judgment to them at any time.

Another way in which judgments can come back on us is that we can become like the person we judge. Our team has counseled a number of people who have had this type of experience. Sometimes a person who grows up in an abusive and dysfunctional home makes an internal commitment or "vow" that runs something like this, "When I have children, I'm not going to treat them like my parents treated me! They were horrible parents!" This kind of vow is typically based upon a harsh judgment against one's parents, regardless of whether the judgment is expressed or is only implicit in nature. Experience in the counseling room suggests that a person who judges their parents in this way often ends up treating their kids in much the same way their parents treated them. Abused kids tend to judge their parents, and kids who judge their parents tend to become abusive parents themselves.

Obviously this is attributable in part to the negative example of their parents, but I suspect it is also due to the impact of bitterness and anger against their parents and the judgments that they made against them. They strive to relate to their kids in a different way in accordance with the "vow" that they have made in their heart. Nevertheless, three factors lead toward failure. First, their source of power is often incorrect. Having vowed in their heart not to become like their parents, they press on in their own power rather than in humble dependence on the Holy Spirit. Second, their reference point is typically wrong. Instead of seeking to become the parent that God would have them to be based on their understanding of Scripture, they react against the parental style used by their own father and mother. Rather than being positively Christ-centered, their concept of being a good parent is the opposite of whatever their parents did. Third, in my experience it seems that this type of inner vow gives demonic powers a chance to work in our lives, and their purpose and intention is never good. Because of these factors, many people fail to fulfill their vow. Though they long to break the abusive cycle, often they are unable to do so until they have first repented of the judgments they have made against their parents and broken the power of these judgments in their lives.

Judgments can cause a loss of blessing in our lives

Any sin that is practiced over time can cause a disruption in the flow of God's blessing in our lives. This is especially true, however, when the sin in question is ongoing and runs contrary to the basic principles of God's Word, as in the case of a judgmental spirit. Believers who are focusing on the speck in their brother's eye are rarely living the abundant life that God desires for them as His children.

While all judgments can disrupt the flow of God's blessings, the most devastating results come when we judge our parents. Why is this? First, such judgments are often made by those who have never experienced the love they need and desire from a parent or parents, but rather neglect, indifference, rejection, cruelty, and abuse. Such treatment is, in itself, exceedingly harmful and usually wounds deeply the child's heart. This is especially true since children lack the capacity to understand that their parents mistreat them because of their own issues and sin, not because the children have done anything wrong or were unworthy of their parents' love.

As if this type of damage is not enough, at some point in a child's development their own defense mechanisms kick in. They may close or harden their hearts toward their parents, reject them, and judge them. They will often set out on a course of rebellion that is both a search for something that will relieve the pain they feel and an attempt to give meaning and significance to their lives. This search may lead them to alcohol, drugs, sex, the occult, false religions, and workaholic tendencies, just to name a few of the possibilities. Once they have embarked on this course, with a judgment on their parents at the very root of their rejection and rebellion, it becomes much more difficult to unravel the web of sin and deceit that keeps them in bondage.

When we do not honor our parents, but instead make judgments in our hearts against them, then we close the door to many of the blessings that God desires to shower on us as His children. It does not "go well with us," yet the root cause of the problem is often hidden from us. We do not realize the judgments we have made.

It is ironic that the people who have the most difficult time admitting and renouncing the judgments they have made against their parents are those who have a fairly positive view of their parents. Often parents are neglectful or abusive when their children are small, but then they repent and accept Christ as their children are growing up, and their lives and their household undergo a dramatic transformation. As time goes on their children also accept Christ and come to appreciate their parents' lives and spiritual commitment. Nevertheless, as these children come to adulthood they experience problems due to the judgments against their parents that were made as children and are still hidden away in their hearts. Often it takes the Holy Spirit's work to open their hearts and to lay bare the judgment that is hidden deep within, and to bring repentance and freedom to the person's life. Still, some people with a fairly positive view of their parents are simply unwilling to explore the possibility that they made a judgment against their parents early in their life, and that this judgment is influencing their life in the present. Such people often do not experience full healing and freedom in Christ.

"Why shouldn't we judge others who hurt us?" For one thing, it should be obvious to the reader that the consequences of making ungodly judgments are serious indeed. Regardless of how horrifying or unjust our circumstances may be, ungodly judgments against God, ourselves, and others only compound our pain and bring us unto bondage. Such consequences are tragic especially since in reality God is there, walking through every trial with us. He is there whispering to us,

> "For I, the LORD your God, will hold your right hand,
> Saying to you, 'Fear not, I will help you.'"
>
> (Isaiah 41:13 NKJV)

How can we judge Him who loves us with an everlasting love, who suffers through our trials with us, and who was willing to give up His own Son's life for us? In the same way, how can we judge ourselves when we read in Scripture that He loves us, that we are "precious and honored" in His sight (Isaiah 43:4)? And how can we make judgments against others when to do so runs contrary to God's will for us as His people? Should we not rather learn to accept each other and to bear with each other, just as the Lord accepts us with all our shortcomings, failings, and sins (Colossians 3:12–14)? To quote the Apostle Paul's words from a slightly different context, do not by making ungodly judgments "destroy your brother for whom Christ died" (Romans 14:15). The consequences that come from making ungodly judgments of any type are heavy indeed, which is why a clear understanding of God's will for His people in this area is essential. And once we know the will of God, there remains only one thing – the final step of obedience.

Notes

1. Chester and Betsy Kylstra, *An Integrated Approach to Biblical Healing Ministry* (Kent, England: Sovereign World, 2003), 169–170, refer to "pouring out our complaint" before the Lord. In my experience, pouring out our hurt and confusion before the Lord is a critical step in the healing process.

2. Giving up the defenses that we have relied upon since childhood is often difficult, and requires a definite step of faith on the part of the counselee. Often there are "guardian lies" that hinder the process, such as "I will be unsafe if I let down my protective walls"; cf. Karl D. Lehman and Charlotte E.T. Lehman, "Judgments and Bitterness as Clutter that Hinders Prayer for Emotional Healing," 19 June 2002 <http://www.kclehman.com>, 2–3. Ultimately, however, each person must learn to rely on God to be their shield and their protector.

3. See, for example, Derek Prince, *Blessing or Curse: You Can Choose* (Grand Rapids: Chosen Books, 2000), 104–120. While such words are not "curses" in a technical sense, they can function pretty much like a curse, opening the person up to demonic influence and oppression. They can also be internalized by the person to whom they are spoken, so that they function as a kind of "self-curse."

4. The relationship between judgments and bitterness is very close. As Lehman and Lehman, observe: "Our perception is that judgments and bitterness usually (always?) go together. We perceive that bitterness requires judgment – you cannot be bitter towards a person unless you first judge him. We have also observed that judgment will usually (always?) be infected with bitterness – if somebody has hurt you, you can't do anything about it, and you judge and condemn her in response to this wound and powerlessness, bitterness will usually (surely?) follow" (1).

5. Dallas Willard, *The Divine Conspiracy* (London: Fount Paperbacks, 1998), speaks of "the law of reciprocity of condemnation" (245–246).

6. Some writers in the area of inner healing cite these verses uncritically in support of the teaching that if we judge others, they will necessarily judge us. Here we must exercise caution. Two questions are relevant: (1) Who is it who will judge us? and (2) When will we be judged?

In answer to the first question, it seems clear to most commentators that "and you will not be judged" uses the divine passive; i.e. if we have a judgmental spirit, it is God who will judge us; cf. I. Howard Marshall, *Commentary on Luke* (Grand Rapids: Eerdmans, 1978), 266, and Joseph A. Fitzmeyer, *The Gospel according to Luke*, vol. 1 (Garden City, NY: Doubleday, 1981), 641. Regarding the second question, the answer is not so clear. In Matthew's version of this saying (7:1–2), the context is clearly eschatological. In Luke's version, however, the matter is not as clear. Certainly an eschatological interpretation is possible, and that element is probably present, but the context seems more proverbial, and may refer to a person's present experience. After all, the Lord may judge people in the present by allowing them to experience the natural consequences of their experiences. As Leon Morris observes, "It is not quite clear whether *you will not be judged* refers to the present judgment of men or the future judgment of God or both. If we are harsh with our judgments on other people we generally find that they return the compliment and we find ourselves widely condemned, whereas if we do not pass judgment on others our neighbors are slow to condemn us. But the words apply also to more permanent consequences. The man who judges others invites the judgment of God upon himself"; *The Gospel According to St. Luke* (Grand Rapids: Eerdmans, 1974), 132.

Chapter 6

BREAKING THE POWER
OF UNGODLY JUDGMENTS

Some time ago my wife counseled a woman who had been deeply wounded and rejected by her mother. She described her mother as controlling, hypocritical, egotistical, totally self-centered, and completely unconcerned about her daughter's welfare. The woman receiving ministry felt that there was no way she could ever have a relationship with her mom, especially now that she was an adult. As they prayed and waited before the Lord, He showed her that her mother did have certain faults, which was not surprising since judgments tend to have an element of truth in them. However, she was definitely *not* the monster that her daughter had created in her mind as she had judged and rejected her. The counselee immediately recognized the subjective nature of the judgment she had made against her mother, and was amazed that it had controlled her perceptions of her character for so many years. My wife was pleased that she had come to this realization, but also knew that forgiving her mother and releasing the judgment she had made against her would be critical steps in her journey toward healing and freedom in Christ.

Recognizing the judgments we have made against others is an important step in breaking their power in our lives and the lives of others, but the reality is that it is only one in a series of steps toward freedom and victory in Christ. In fact, if all we do is recognize that we have sinned by making judgments against others, but we do nothing about it, we are very much like that man in James 1:22–25 who looks at his face in a mirror, but then goes away and immediately forgets what he looks like. We have become hearers of the word but not doers of it. If, however, we act on the realization that the Holy Spirit has created within us, then we will enjoy the freedom and victory that God desires for each of us in Christ Jesus.

The steps required to break the power of ungodly judgments in our lives and the lives of others are simple and straightforward. All that is required is a humble desire to give up and surrender to God our attitudes that are displeasing to Him, and a willingness to exercise the authority that we possess as believers in the Lord Jesus Christ. It is important as we follow these steps to remember that we should be sensitive to the leading of the Holy Spirit rather than simply working our way through the process in a mechanical fashion. Sometimes the Spirit leads us to vary the order of the steps, or He may bring up other matters that are not included here. For example, in some cases prayer for forgiveness must take place before prayer that God will reveal His truth in a person's heart, thus destroying the power of deep-rooted deceptions that are holding them in bondage. The basic principle is one of flexibility. The Lord knows better than anyone the deepest needs of our hearts, and He is willing to show us the way to healing and wholeness, provided we are ready to follow His leading.

We confess the sin of judging the other person and receive God's forgiveness

When we make judgments against another person or group of people, we tend to focus on the sin that they have committed against us. As a result, we feel a certain righteousness in our position as judge. The road to freedom and victory requires, however, that we give up our judgment against them. This does not mean that we must pretend that the person has never wronged us, or that we are blind to their faults. What it does mean is that we must give proper attention to our own wrong attitude and confess as sin the judgment we have made in our heart against them. It does not matter what they have done to us, whether in word or deed. The chances are that they have hurt us pretty badly. Yet we are not responsible for another person's sinful attitudes or behavior. That's between them and God. We are, however, responsible for our own attitudes and behavior. If we want to be free, then we must take responsibility for the judgment we have made in our heart and confess it as sin to God.

Once we have confessed the judgment we have made against the other person, then we should take the additional step of receiving God's forgiveness by faith. In my experience it is valuable to think of God's promise in 1 John 1:9:

> If we confess our sins, he is faithful and just and will forgive us our sins and purify us from all unrighteousness.

According to this conditional promise, we who come to God with sincere hearts to confess our sins (including our judgments) can be confident of His willingness to forgive us. This forgiveness does not have anything to do with salvation, but is relational in nature. If God has forgiven us, then we can approach Him confidently, knowing that there is nothing standing in the way of our enjoying His love and care for us.

It is critical that we receive and enjoy God's forgiveness so that we are not haunted by false guilt or the accusations of the Evil One. I remember asking one Christian woman if she had ever confessed the sin that she had committed at one time to the Lord, and I'll never forget her answer. "I confess it every day!" she exclaimed. She understood clearly the need to confess her sin to the Lord, but had yet to grasp the importance of receiving and enjoying His forgiveness. Just imagine if I had wronged a friend in some way. How would he feel if I came to him day after day, confessing the same sin over and over? Once I confessed the matter to him, and he forgave my sin, the matter should have been settled. I mention this matter because some people are appalled when they realize that they have been harboring the sin of bitterness and making ungodly judgments for most of their life. In such cases confession of sin is critical, but we must also receive and enjoy God's forgiveness.

While confessing our sin and receiving God's forgiveness is a critical first step in breaking the power of ungodly judgments, we must take care to deal with the roots of the problem so that we are truly set free from the judgment's power. This leads us naturally from repentance to the revelation and application of the truth that sets us free.

We ask the Lord to show us areas of deception that undergird the judgment and to reveal His truth in our hearts

In many cases a deception is at the root of judgments that we make against individuals and groups. Sometimes this deception is primarily intellectual and will respond to wise counsel and biblical instruction. In such cases, we listen attentively to the person discuss their feelings about a particular person or group to see if we detect a judgment against them. If we do, we prayerfully discern the deception that anchors or undergirds the judgment, using the criteria that were outlined in chapter 2. Once we have identified the lie (e.g. "All men are dogs"), then we can help the person understand the nature of the deception, and use biblical and experiential truth to neutralize its power in their life (e.g. by showing that men are created by God and loved by Him, and besides it is not fair to lump them all together). This approach is used by advocates of Christian forms of cognitive therapy, including those who combine this approach with teaching on spiritual warfare.[1]

A typical dialogue using this type of approach to the lie that "All men are dogs" might run as follows:

Counselor: So you feel that men are dirty, that they're disgusting, that they just want to have sex with anyone?

Counselee: Yeah, that's it. I just feel like they're dogs.

Counselor: I can certainly understand how you might feel that way given your experiences with certain men. Certainly there are some men who aren't worthy of your trust. Still, do you think it's fair to lump them all together? Do you think all men are the same?

Counselee: I guess not. It's just that I've felt that way. I think I've been afraid to open up to them. I'm afraid I'll be hurt again just like I was in the past.

Counselor: I can certainly understand your feelings. As a Christian, what do think the Bible teaches about men, not a particular man but men in general?

Counselee: I guess God created them just like He did women.

Counselor: That's right. Does God love them?

Counselee: Yes.

Counselor: Did Christ die for them just like He did for women?

Counselee: Yes.

Counselor: Is the Holy Spirit at work in believing men just as He is in women?

Counselee: Sure.

Counselor: Do you think, then, that it's true that "all men are dogs"?

Counselee: No, I don't think it is.

Counselor: Do you think you're ready to give up that deception?

Counselee: I think I am.

Counselor: Great! Do you think you can bring it to the Lord in prayer, confessing that you've believed a lie about men, and renounce it openly before Him?

Counselee: I'm ready. [The counselee prays, confessing and renouncing the lie about men.]

Counselor: Now I'd like to make a declaration. Based on your confession and renunciation of the deception that "all men are dogs," I break the power of this judgment in your life, in Jesus' name.

In many cases this approach is quite effective and leads to the breaking of the power of the deception that anchors and reinforces a particular judgment. In other cases, however, the deception is deeply rooted in a person's heart and will only respond to a powerful work of the Spirit in the context of healing prayer. During this type of ministry, Jesus Himself reveals His truth in the heart of the person and effectively destroys the deception that was at the root of the judgment. After the deception has been cleared away, the person can move forward in the process of breaking the power of the judgment in their lives.

A missionary (whom we will call Jenny), whose parents were unable to give her the love and affection that she needed as a small child, was angry with God as a result of the deeply rooted deception that "No one was there to care for her." She felt that God had let her down by placing her in such a messed-up family and had judged Him to be uncaring as well. As my wife prayed with her, asking the Lord if there was anything He wanted to show her about her belief that "No one was there to care for her," He immediately reminded her of her grandmother's love. Here is what happened:

Counselor: So, Jenny, from your reaction as we prayed, it seems the Lord showed you something. What did you just experience?

Counselee: I saw myself sitting in a car, but someone else was with me.

Counselor: Why was it?

Counselee: I'm not sure.

Counselor: Let's go to the Lord again in prayer and ask Him to show us. OK? Lord, would You show Jenny who was there in the car with her?

Counselee: It was my grandmother! You know, she often took me with her, and she was really good to me. We really did a lot of things together.

Counselor: Is that realization helpful to you?

Counselee: Yes, it is. I believe Jesus is showing me that I've been wrong. I wasn't really alone. He knew I needed someone to love me, so He gave me my grandmother. It's like He loved me through her.

Counselor: Great! Is there anything you'd like to say to the Lord in response to this realization?

Counselee: Yes, there is. I've been mad at Him for no reason. I need to confess that to Him.

Counselor: Have you also judged Him in your heart?

Counselee: Yes, I have! I judged Him to be uncaring, when in fact He was always looking out for me!

Counselor: Would you like to confess to Him your anger and your judgment?

Counselee: Yes, I would...

In cases such as these, this type of revelation from Jesus Himself can bring lasting freedom from feelings of anger and the sense of being alone in a way that simply cannot be achieved through discussion, teaching, and exhortation. Patient, gentle prayer ministry of this kind can bring healing that reaches not only to the mind, but also to the heart.

Though the ministry approach we use may vary from case to case, the fact is that judgments are often anchored by deep-level lies or deceptions. Many examples of this type of deception can be cited. When we judge individuals, the judgment typically rests on our false assumption that we are innocent by comparison or that our sin is not as heinous as theirs. Or we may lose perspective on the person so that their sins, failings or weaknesses begin to define them in our thinking. Instead of seeing the person as they really are, with both strengths and weaknesses, we begin to see them one-dimensionally and, ultimately, to vilify them. We may also assume that a person has hurt or offended us intentionally when in fact they never intended to do us any harm, and may not even realize that they hurt or offended us. The reality is that we may be completely mistaken in our assessment of their motives.

In cases where our judgment has generalized to include the entire group that is represented by the person or persons who have wounded or offended us, the deception is often simple. We attribute to all members of the group the negative characteristics that we have observed in the life of the person or persons who wounded us. The truth is that not all men or women or blacks or Hispanics or people in authority over us are the same. The fact that we were hurt or offended by one person does not mean that we must distance ourselves from every person in that group in order to avoid being hurt. Often these types of deceptions can be deeply rooted in our emotions, especially when they develop as a result of traumas that occurred early in our lives.

As I have observed in previous chapters, judgments against God often have their roots in deceptions that originated in traumatic experiences from the past. An abusive childhood, a chronic illness, the loss of a loved one – these kinds of traumatic experiences can be interpreted as indications that God is cruel or sadistic, that He will abandon us in times of trouble, or that He just does not really care about us. Often these false interpretations grow out of expectations that are unfounded. We expect God to act in certain ways (in spite of the fact that He never promised to act that way), then we judge Him when He does not act in accordance with our expectations. For example, some believers assume that God will always heal a loved one who is sick, then interpret the death of a loved one as evidence that He does not really care about us. Or we might assume that the Lord will open the way for us to marry a person we love, then draw the conclusion that God cannot be trusted if the other person chooses to break off the relationship. Deep-level deceptions such as these often form the basis for judgments that block our experience of intimacy with God and hinder our progress in spiritual growth. In fact, they drive a wedge between us and the Source of true healing and wholeness. For this reason, we often say that our first priority in counseling with many people is helping them realize deep within their heart that God really is on their team.

Deep-level deception can also be at the root of judgments against ourselves. Often critical words spoken by others and traumatic experiences of rejection lead us to believe – deep within our hearts – that we are dirty, shameful, stupid, destined for failure, unworthy, or unlovable. Believers who are in the grip of this type of deception and the resulting judgments they have made toward themselves are typically unable to grasp their holiness in Christ, their gifts and abilities, and the fact that they have been made worthy in God's Son. And since they do not have a true sense of their identity in Christ, they often struggle not only in their relationship to God and themselves but also in their relationships with others.

As with judgments in general, the approach must be tailored to the needs of each individual. In some cases, it is enough to teach them informally about God's love and grace, and their value to the Heavenly Father, and to model that same love in our interactions with them, so that they experience unconditional love in their relationship with us. However, as I mentioned earlier, certain deceptions can also be buried deep within their heart, in which case they will not respond well to reason and instruction. The person may already believe the truth with their mind, but somehow the deception still controls their feelings and influences their reactions in certain situations. In such cases, we must bring them to the Lord in prayer and allow Him to reveal His love and truth in their heart. Then we must wait patiently for the Lord to work. In some cases He works very quickly, and in a few seconds the person receiving prayer experiences God's love in their inner man, while in other cases the process can take several minutes. The important thing is to pray gently and patiently, and to wait for the Lord to reveal the truth that the person needs. He often does this in creative and surprising ways, as we pray in line with Paul's petition in Ephesians 3:17b–19a:

> And I pray that you, being rooted and established in love, may have power, together with all the saints, to grasp how wide and long and high and deep is the love of Christ, and to know this love that surpasses knowledge...

When God reveals His love (or other important truths) to a person in this way, deceptions regarding His nature and character, as well as lies that relate to their position and worth before God, are destroyed, and the transformation that takes place in their life, their relationship with God, and their relationship to others can be truly amazing. In my experience, God loves to reveal His tender love in this way, especially to His children who have been rejected and abused.

We choose to forgive the wrongs the other person has committed against us – which involves releasing the judgment we have made against them

If we have made a judgment against another person because their words or their actions have wounded us, then the next step we need to take is forgiveness. We need to release to the

Lord our feelings of hurt, anger, or bitterness, as well as any judgments we have made against them and our right to revenge. This means consciously letting go of these things and opening up our hearts to God's healing love and grace. Only then can we experience true freedom and victory in Christ.

How exactly do we do release the feelings and the judgments that hold us in bondage? The first thing we must do is make sure our heart, or the heart of someone to whom we are ministering, is truly ready to forgive. It is easy to forgive at a superficial level, but the forgiveness that God desires from us, the forgiveness that really sets us free, comes "from the heart" (Matthew 18:35). Often we must spend some time in prayer, allowing the Holy Spirit to soften and prepare our hearts to forgive, before we can step out and release the bitterness that holds us in bondage. In counseling sessions with others who are struggling with the desire to forgive, but who are ready to allow the Holy Spirit to soften and prepare their hearts for this big step, we often spend some time praying quietly and waiting for the Lord to do His preparatory work before we move into the process of forgiveness. In most cases this prayer ministry is very effective, but sometimes we need to wait until the next ministry session before attempting to lead them in prayer to forgive the one who hurt or offended them.

When the person receiving ministry is ready to move ahead in the process, it is often helpful to have them pour out their heart to the Lord, expressing their pain and hurt honestly and openly before Him. We then give them permission to mention specific words and actions that have hurt them deeply. This is the time for them to pour out their feelings of anger, disappointment, and betrayal, both toward the Lord and toward the individual who wounded them. Sometimes the counselee will be surprised at the feelings that surface during this stage of the ministry. Often tears flow as they release emotions that have been pushed down or denied since the hurtful events occurred. These tears are frequently a critical element in the healing process. This process must not be rushed. The person needs plenty of time to express their pain.

After someone has poured out their heart before the Lord, it is time for them to go to prayer to release their bitterness, the judgments they have made, and their right to revenge. Whether we are doing this for ourselves or leading another person in the process of forgiveness, the prayer should go something like this:

> Heavenly Father, You know my pain. You know how much _____'s words and actions hurt me. I do not come to justify what _____ did, but to forgive him/her for it. I now open my wounded and angry heart before You, and I release to You all the negative feelings – the anger and the bitterness – that I feel toward _____. I also release any judgments that I have made against _____, as well as my right to revenge. I know that only You have the right to judge, and that You will do it justly.
>
> In addition to releasing these things to You, I also ask that You come now and fill my heart. Where there has been bitterness, fill me with love for _____. Where there has been turmoil, fill me with peace. Where there has been sadness and peace, fill me with joy.
>
> I choose to forgive _____ for his/her words and his/her actions. Give me strength to walk in forgiveness toward him/her each day while You bring to completion Your healing work in me. In Jesus' name, Amen.[2]

When believers truly release their anger and bitterness, their judgments, and their right to revenge – in short, when they choose to forgive from the heart – they often experience a deep sense of relief. Counselees often report a lightness of spirit and a renewed sense of joy when they choose to forgive those who have hurt them. Yet forgiveness is not only a choice that we make at one point in time, it is also a process in which we must choose to walk day by day. It is common, for example, for feelings of anger that have been surrendered to the Lord to pop up again in certain situations. At those times we can simply go to the Lord in prayer and confess our need for His continued help and grace:

> Heavenly Father, I've already forgiven _____, but here these feelings are again. I release them to You, and choose to walk in the path of forgiveness. Lord, continue Your healing work in me, for Your glory and honor. Amen.

As we choose the way of forgiveness and walk in it, we experience a gradual change in our feelings and perceptions toward the other person. We find ourselves experiencing the healing and restoration that only God can bring.

In relation to the need for forgiveness, I often find that believers do not understand the close connection between the wounds that others inflict upon us and the judgments that we make against them. The reality is that we frequently make judgments against others who have hurt or offended us. In fact, it is usually a hurt or offense that drives us to make ungodly judgments against others. As a result, we only truly forgive another person when we release our hurts and offenses as well as let go of the judgments we have made against another person. Both aspects of the forgiveness process are critical.

In this way forgiving someone for the wrong that they have committed against us and releasing the judgment that we have made against them are often two sides of the same coin. It is difficult to imagine how we can truly forgive someone "from the heart" – releasing all the anger and bitterness that we have stored up against them – and still hold on to ungodly judgments against them. On the other hand, it is impossible to repent of the judgments that we have made against another person if we have not released the anger and the bitterness that we are holding against them. The two aspects of the process are intimately related yet still distinct. Forgiveness relates to the feelings that are stored up within us, while releasing judgments relates to our attitude, our mindset, and our expectations toward the person who has wounded us. Once again, both aspects are critical if we are to enjoy freedom and victory in Christ.

In some cases, the two aspects of the process are resolved by what seems to be a single work of the Spirit. As we release our negative feelings to the Lord, we also repent of the ungodly judgments we have made against the people who have hurt or offended us. In other cases, however, the distinction between the two aspects of the process is noticeable. This is especially true when judgments have generalized. For example, a woman may have forgiven her brother and father as individuals for molesting her, yet still distance herself from the opposite sex because of a judgment against men in general that is buried deep within her heart. In other cases she may find that she experiences difficulty in forgiving completely individual men because of the influence of a judgment against all men that is still unresolved in her life. Discerning the proper order in this type of ministry requires discernment, experience and, at times, trial and error.

We use our spiritual authority to break the power of the judgment in our lives and in the lives of others

Judgments that we have made in our hearts, as well as those that have been made by others against us, can influence our lives in powerful ways. Many times this negative influence results from the trauma of the words that were spoken against us. For example, a parent's judgment against his child, expressed in the words "You'll never amount to anything!", can lodge deep in the heart of that child and influence the entire course of his life. It can influence his self-concept, leading him to fear challenges and to expect failure in all that he does. Often the parent's "prophecy" becomes self-fulfilling.

There is, however, a deeper, spiritual dimension to the power of judgments that we should not ignore. Just like unresolved anger, bitterness, and hatred, judgments can also give Satan an "opportunity" to work in our lives (Ephesians 4:26–27), and we can be sure that his work is never to our benefit! This is true both of judgments we have made against others and judgments that others have made against us. The enemy will use the opportunity we have given him to undermine our relationship with God and with other people, to disrupt the unity of the body of Christ, and to keep our ministries from bearing fruit to God's glory.

What can we do to break the power of judgments in our lives and the lives of others? To some extent this depends on the situation. If we have made a judgment against another person, we must confess the judgment we have made and release it to the Lord, and then we should use our authority in Jesus Christ to break the power of the judgment in our life and in the life of the one against whom it was made.[3] We can do this by declaring,

> In the name of Jesus my Lord I break the power of the judgment I have made against _____, both in my life and in his/her life. I declare in the heavenlies that the power of this judgment is broken, and that no spiritual powers may use it against him/her or against me. Amen.

Please remember that it is not the exact words of the declaration that are important, but rather the substance. Whether we feel a difference immediately or not, God often uses this kind of authoritative declaration to set us free from the power of sinful judgments we have made against others.

What do we do, however, when others have made judgments against us? In these cases we must reject the words of the judgment against us, affirm God's truth, and then make a declaration like the following:

> In the name of Jesus my Lord I break the power of the
> judgment that was made against me by _____, namely
> that I [*insert the content of the judgment*]. I declare in the heavenlies
> that the power of this judgment is broken, and that no spiritual
> powers may use it against him/her or against me. Amen.

In the case of the judgment mentioned above, i.e. that we will
not amount to anything, we should pray to reject these words,
affirm that "we can do all things through Christ who strengthens us," and then make the declaration breaking the power of
the judgment. The process is simple and can be performed by
any true believer in the Lord Jesus Christ.

We command any spirits who are at work in our lives through the judgments we have made – or the judgments of others against us – to leave

Once we have broken the power of a judgment in our lives,
there only remains the simple step of commanding any spirits
that may be present as a result of the judgment to leave. This
principle may be new to some readers, who are unaccustomed
to thinking in terms of demonic influence in the lives of
believers, or who have never directly challenged the powers
of darkness. I cannot at this point give a detailed explanation
and defense of this teaching; for that the reader should consult
one of several works that discuss the biblical and theological
evidence in some detail.[4] However, experience has shown that
demonic forces can work in and through the judgments that we
make against God, ourselves, and others. For this reason, the
additional step of commanding demonic forces that are at work
in our lives, or in the lives of those to whom we are ministering,
to leave, is an important part of resolving the influence of
ungodly judgments.

By this point in the ministry process deliverance should be
relatively easy. To use Charles Kraft's illustration, once the

trash (i.e. judgment) is eliminated, the rats (i.e. evil spirits) should go without too much of a struggle.[5] Still, in many cases, we need to exercise our authority in Christ to command them to leave.

After completing the steps listed above, I recommend that you give a direct command to any evil spirits who are working in your life or another person's life as follows:

> In the name of our Lord and Savior Jesus Christ, I command any spirits that are at work in _____'s life due to the judgment that he/she made against _____ to leave him/ her immediately and never to return. He/she has repented of this judgment and broken its power in his/her life, so you have no grounds on which to continue your evil work in his/her life. You must leave now.

If there are indications that the judgment has been passed down from the mother or father, I recommend that you cut any unhealthy ties that exist between you and your parents, or the person and their parents, then command any spirits that were passed down to you or them to leave immediately:

> In the name of our Lord and Savior Jesus Christ, I break any unhealthy ties between _____ and his/her [*father or mother*]. I also command any spirits that were passed down to him/her as a result of his/her [*father's or mother's*] judgment toward _____ to leave immediately and never to return.

Once again, it is not necessary to repeat these words exactly as written. It is rather the substance of the declaration and command that is important.

Continue to challenge the spirits for some time – say at least two to three minutes. I recommend that you place the spirits under the authority that you have in Christ and forbid them to hide or to pretend they are not there. Remind them that you (or the person to whom you are ministering) have confessed the judgment, renounced it, and broken its power. Therefore, they have no grounds for continuing their evil work of reinforcing the negative impact of the judgment. This simple process may feel strange the first time you do it. At least it did to me! After all, it may turn out that no demons are present! Yet experience has shown that strong judgments often serve as an anchor for demonic influence. If there are no manifestations after several minutes, you can stop. The lack of any manifestations usually means (1) that there were no spirits present, (2) that the spirits who were present already left quietly during the earlier steps, or (3) that the spirits just left, but without manifesting in any way.

If the person receiving ministry experiences manifestations such as unusual thoughts (e.g. demons screaming in their thoughts that they aren't going to leave), or unusual physical symptoms (e.g. pain in a part of their body, dizziness, coughing, or retching), simply continue to challenge the spirits until the symptoms stop. You can also forbid them to harm the person in any way. If you have already followed the previous steps, then any spirits that are at work in their life because of the judgment should leave.

After that I would recommend praying for the person, asking God's protection and leading so that they will walk in freedom from the judgments that have held them in bondage. The goal of the ministry is to help the person grow in Christ and to continue to live in accordance with God's will for their life.

We make right the wrongs we have committed as a result of our judgment against the person in question

It is important to mention that in many cases we must act to right the wrongs we have committed as a result of the judgments we have made. I say "in many cases" because some judgments are primarily internal. Judgments always hinder our relationship with the Lord, but at times we do not hurt or offend other people based on the judgments we have made against them. In those cases it is sufficient to confess our judgment to God, renounce it, and break its power in our lives. In other situations, however, we have assumed the worst of others, interpreted their actions in negative ways, imputed sinful motives to them, made hurtful or offensive comments, or distanced ourselves from another person based on the judgments we have made against them or the groups they represent. In such cases our sinful beliefs and attitudes have led us to sin against them, and we should act to put right the wrongs we have committed.

In situations where our judgments have led us to hurt or offend others, whenever it is practical and possible we should go directly to the person and attempt to make things right. This is in line with the biblical teaching that we should confess our sins to each other (James 5:16), as well as Jesus' teaching on the importance of reconciliation:

> "Therefore, if you are offering your gift at the altar and there remember that your brother has something against you, leave your gift there in front of the altar. First go and be reconciled to your brother; then come and offer your gift."
>
> (Matthew 5:23–24)

The Lord stresses the importance of this step by teaching that reconciliation should take priority even over worship. If we have sinned against our brother and he has something against us, then we should go to him … quickly! When we go, we should apologize for our behavior and ask his forgiveness. Whether or not we mention the judgment we made against him is a matter that requires wisdom. What is critical, however, is that we take responsibility for our own sin and do not imply that his sin drove us to it. Once we own up to our sin and ask his forgiveness, then the ball is in his court. Whether or not full reconciliation takes place is now up to him. The important thing is that we have done what we can, having traveled as far as possible down the road that leads to reconciliation. As the Apostle Paul wrote,

> If it is possible, as far as it depends on you, live at peace with everyone.
>
> (Romans 12:18)

Some time ago I counseled a young woman who had broken up with her boyfriend due to the influence of a judgment on men. Though she loved him a lot and felt he was the kind of man she would like to marry, something in her drove her to break up with him. This hurt him deeply as he also loved her and was deeply committed to their relationship. In counseling, we realized that she had made a judgment against men based on the fact that her dad had mistreated her, and that this judgment had driven her to break up with him. In the ministry session she was set free from the power of that judgment, yet she needed to do one more thing. She needed to apologize to her ex-boyfriend for hurting him and explain what happened.

Not every situation is the same. In some cases it is impossible to confess our sins to those we have hurt. For example, the person may have died, we may have lost contact with them so that further contact is impossible, or we may feel that confession would only make things worse given the person's attitudes and perceptions of the situation. In such cases we can only bring the matter to the Lord and follow the steps to freedom from the judgment we made at one time. That will be enough. We must not give the devil an opportunity to accuse us because certain things remain undone, especially when those things are impossible given our current situation.

We make a commitment in our heart not to judge other people ... with Christ's help!

If we want to enjoy the abundant life that God has planned for us, then we must not only repent of the judgments that we have made against others in the past, but we must also make a commitment not to fall into this trap in the future. Why is this critical? It is critical because the chances are that sooner or later we will be wounded or offended by someone at home, at church, at school, at work, or elsewhere. That is just a part of being human, and if we are not careful, we can judge others without even realizing it. If, however, we are aware of the danger of judging others and make a commitment in our hearts to avoid doing so, then when the hurts and disappointments come we can stand firm in obedience to our Lord. The eight questions I suggested in chapter 2 can help us evaluate our relationships and our responses so that we can avoid falling into ungodly judgments.

Knowing freedom in the area of judging others is both an event and a process. When we renounce the judgments we have made, confess them as sin, receive the Lord's forgiveness, and break the power of the judgments we have made, we take a huge step toward living in freedom and victory in Christ. Nevertheless, we must choose to "walk it out" by forgiving others who wrong us, praying regularly for them, and choosing to leave judgment in God's hand. At first this is a challenge ... believe me! As we do this on a regular basis, however, we form new patterns of thinking, responding, and relating to others. Over time the process will become easier and more natural to us. It will become a new lifestyle for us. Only then will we truly know and experience the abundant life that God desires for us.

Notes

1. See, for example, the books by William Backus, including *Telling the Truth to Troubled People* (Minneapolis: Bethany House, 1985). This is also the type of deception that is effectively countered by Neil Anderson's "truth encounter"; see, for example, *The Bondage Breaker* (Eugene, OR: Harvest House, 2000), and *Victory over the Darkness* (Ventura, CA: Regal Books, 2000). This approach to discipleship, counseling, and spiritual warfare is increasingly common in the Church today; see Kenneth Copley, *The Great Deceiver* (Chicago: Moody Press, 2001).

2. The danger in providing a sample prayer of this type is that the reader will regard it as a kind of magic formula that must be followed, rather as a pattern that may be adapted to one's own situation and personality. In the end, we must remember that God is far more concerned with our hearts than He is with our words.

3. Our authority to break the power of judgments, just like our power to break the power of curses and to oppose the influence of evil spirits, comes from our position in Christ; see Charles H. Kraft, *I Give You Authority* (East Sussex, England: Monarch Books, 1998). Such authority is not a particular spiritual gift, but is the possession of each and every person who is truly "in Christ."

4. See, again, Clinton E. Arnold, *3 Crucial Questions about Spiritual Warfare* (Grand Rapids, MI: Baker Books, 1997), 17–141; cf. the full-length treatments by C. Fred Dickason, *Demon Possession and the Christian* (Chicago: Moody Press, 1987), and Merrill F. Unger, *What Demons Can Do To Saints* (Chicago: Moody Press, 1991); also, Ed Murphy, *The Handbook of Spiritual Warfare* (Nashville: Thomas Nelson, 1992), 429–462.

5. See, for example, Charles H. Kraft, *Defeating Dark Angels* (Ann Arbor, MI: Servant Publications, 1992), 78.

Chapter 7

UPROOTING JUDGMENTS: SOME MINISTRY ACCOUNTS

In addition to studying the biblical teachings on ungodly judgments and the application of these principles in our lives, it is also helpful to hear the testimonies of believers whose lives have changed radically since they have renounced ungodly judgments. I would like to share three accounts of ministry with you, one representing a judgment primarily against God, one depicting a judgment against self, and the final one illustrating a judgment against others. By reading these accounts, it is my hope that the reader will understand the tremendous power of God to uproot the judgments in our lives and to set us free from their negative influence.

A judgment against God

Mary came to us in some confusion about the nature of God's love. She was a part of a program that focused on growth in spiritual discernment and maturity, but was finding that she was having trouble accepting the biblical teaching that God loved her. In fact, she described that whenever anyone would tell her that God loved her or read her Scripture that attested to that fact she would feel resistance to that idea. Sometimes she would even tune the speaker out. She felt that to attest to God's love would be similar to repeating a mantra. She didn't want to simply repeat the words over and over until they seemed true. She indicated to us that until she felt the words to be true she didn't feel comfortable saying or hearing them.

As we listened to Mary's life history and heard her describe her family dynamics it became clear that she came from a background where love was conditional and the way to earn love was to produce. Mary was the only child of an overly controlling, driven mother and a passive father who cautioned her to try not to rock the boat. Mary was home-schooled and expected to be perfect in every aspect of life. If she transgressed in any way, no matter how insignificant, she was forced to apologize to both of her parents as well as to God. Mary graduated from high school at the age of sixteen and immediately left home for college where she was enrolled in an honor's program which exacerbated her driven-ness and perfectionism. By this time she had lost any sense of intimacy with God and felt that although God had loved her in the past, He didn't love her in the present.

As we prayed about these issues with Mary the Lord revealed two important keys. One was that Mary was trying to win her way into heaven with her good behavior, by doing everything "right." The Lord showed Mary a picture of Jesus on the cross and herself pushing the cross away. She had trouble accepting that Jesus had done all that was necessary for her to be received by His Father. She struggled to believe that she didn't have to do everything right for the Father to love her. She wanted to earn God's love and approbation through all of the good things she was doing. Even though she had confessed the sin in her life that seemed most devastating to her, she did not believe that she could accept God's forgiveness. She was still trying to make up for falling into sin in a particular area of her life. As she described it to us, she felt that when she chose to sin in that way, God "dumped" her. It wasn't enough that Jesus had died to cleanse her from sin, she was still trying to make up for "throwing God's goodness in His face" by sinning the way she did.

After some more prayer, the Lord made it clear that Mary also had a judgment on Him. She didn't believe that God could love her "in her bad" – in those areas where she still struggled with sin and was less than perfect. She didn't believe that He was as good as His word, that He would accept her as she was.

As we prayed through Mary's resistance to God's love and acceptance He spoke to her through the image of the woman caught in adultery in John 8:1–11. First the Lord spoke to her about her desire to make things right with Him through her own efforts. He pointed out that the Pharisees who had brought the woman to Jesus were convinced of their own righteousness and ability to achieve reconciliation with God through their own efforts. They were trying to be acceptable to God "in their good." Jesus made it plain that they were in no condition to condemn the sinner and in fact were not able to receive God's love because of their pride. The Lord then revealed that apart from Him Mary was just like the woman brought before Jesus for judgment. Jesus knew the woman had committed adultery. He knew that according to Mosaic law she should have been stoned to death, but He accepted her "in her bad." She didn't have to do anything to be received by Jesus; all she had to do was respond to His love. In the same way, God the Father loved Mary in the midst of her sin and struggles, and all He asked of her was that she respond to His love instead of refusing to believe that He would offer it to her.

After that revelation, Mary was able to release her judgment on God and accept the truth that He loved her quite apart from anything she might do or how she might serve Him. She has been excited to hear about God's love and now finds it refreshing and renewing to contemplate how much God loves her. She is enjoying a new freedom to receive God's love and believe what the Scripture tells her to be true concerning our

Father's heart toward all of His children. She also knows that she needs to keep growing and experiencing healing in different areas of her life based on her new understanding of God and His relationship to her.

A judgment against self

One Christian worker had been haunted by feelings of inadequacy all of her life. It always seemed that no matter how hard she tried to do something well it was never good enough. The phrase "I just can't get it right" was a reoccurring theme in her thoughts and often led her to tears. One Sunday she was headed to church with her family when she realized that her teenage son was not satisfied with some plans that she had made. She felt that she had worked exceptionally hard to figure everything out in a way that would be acceptable to every member of her family. However, the fact that he was not pleased caused the old, familiar feelings of inadequacy to well up within her. As her son and daughter left the car and began walking into church, she started to cry, thinking to herself, "I just can't get it right, I try so hard, but I just can't get it right." At that point, her husband intervened. He turned the car around and told her that they were going to seek the Lord about this matter instead of allowing it to keep controlling her.

After a time in prayer the Lord revealed to her that she had a judgment on herself. She had judged herself as a failure. When they asked the Lord to reveal to them the root of the self-judgment, she was surprised by the memory that surfaced. She saw herself again taking part in her first dance class when she was five years old. She loved to dance, but was not the most svelte of children. She felt comfortable in the ballet part of the class, but less comfortable with the tap and tumbling. When they were told they were going to have a recital which included both tap and ballet, she started feeling scared. She was afraid she was going to look stupid, that the other children would make fun of her, that everyone would know that she couldn't do it right. She had allowed the fear of failure to control her, and it was still coloring her life forty years later!

Through prayer she confessed to the Lord that she had been allowing that fear to dictate her attitude and actions. She told Him that she wanted to be rid of it and renounced all of its effects in her life. Then she asked the Lord to reveal His truth to her about the situation and to reveal Himself to her in whatever way He wished. Soon after that she had a picture of herself in her recital costume, with her tap shoes on. Standing next to her was the Lord Jesus, dressed in a robe but with a top hat on His head, tap shoes on His feet, and a cane in His hands. He turned to her with a delighted smile on His face and asked, "Ready?" When she nodded her head, "yes," she joined Jesus in tap dancing across the stage – sort of shuffling off to Buffalo. He seemed to be having a lot of fun in the process! Her heart was filled with the knowledge that she didn't face any of her trials alone, that the Lord was always with her, and that with Him, she could do whatever needed to be done. It was a richly satisfying moment.

After recounting the vision to her somewhat hysterical spouse, they turned to another aspect of her self-judgment. She grew up in a highly competitive, highly performance-oriented family. Her dad was a classic workaholic and they were always expected to perform at a high level. Love was not conditional; they knew that they were loved no matter what kind of grades they earned or how proficient they became in other areas, but it was expected that their performance would be above average. Because of her fear of failure and her self-judgment she had opted out of the performance mode, but always felt guilty that she wasn't performing at a higher standard. A time of confession and forgiveness led into a breaking of generational ties with her dad's family, from whom she had inherited these tendencies. After a time of deliverance, she felt a lifting of her spirits and a new peace in her heart. The proof that she had been freed from these old patterns came soon afterwards when she had another run-in with her teenage son. She was able to listen to his disappointment about the matter they were discussing without feeling responsible for his problem. She could see that she had done all that she could to make things easier for him and if that wasn't enough (in his eyes), then that was his issue, not hers! What a relief that was to her!

The next year the Lord took her deeper into a related issue. In addition to feeling that she just couldn't get it right, she also had the conviction that although she was one of God's children, she wasn't one of His really special ones. She knew that He loved her, and at times experienced that truth in her heart, but at most other times she felt that He was far off and not too intimately involved in her everyday life. She had undergone ministry before in this area, but still had a hard time experiencing God's presence and unconditional love.

As a part of a conference she attended, she sought the Lord about this issue during a small group time. With several other women praying for her, she asked the Lord to reveal the root of her problem. He brought about a growing conviction that her understanding of her relationship with Him was based on her relationship with her father, a man who loved her but whose time and attention were focused on business. To a certain extent she already knew this to be true, but had been frustrated by the fact that she didn't seem to be able to get beyond the knowledge that this was true, to receiving healing in that area.

The leader of the small group led her in forgiving her father for not being able to give her all that she needed as she was growing up, and then they asked the Lord to bring the truth deep into her heart. Soon she saw a picture of herself as a little girl getting ready for bed, only it was not her mother walking her through her bedtime routine, it was Jesus. He sat next to her while she took a bath, then He dried her with a big fluffy towel and helped her into her pajamas. After overseeing the tooth brushing, He tucked her in her bed. She remembered that during all this activity she didn't stop talking to Him, although she had no idea what she talked about. No doubt she was giving Him a blow by blow run-down of her day. After He tucked her in, the lights turned down low and He sat down in a chair next to her bed. At this point she told Him that He didn't need to stay with her any longer because she was just going to sleep. He replied that He had nowhere else to go, He was content to just sit with her while she slept. She felt warm, loved and protected.

After the small group time, she was involved in a large group meeting that touched her heart deeply as well. But every time she closed her eyes or prayed she was immediately transported back to that quiet, dark room where she could see the Lord simply sitting at her side while she slept. What a beautiful truth that applied to her heart: the Lord had nothing He would rather do than be with her. The judgment she had on herself and in some respect on the Lord was broken and she found it much easier to feel God's love.

A judgment against others

One missionary wife, whose name was Lisa, was struggling in many areas of her life. One area that caused her pain was her inability to work with men and to open her heart to her husband. She related to us that anytime she was upset or angry about something a man did, she would think things like, "You're an idiot!" or "Typical man!", or even worse, "I hate you and wish you were dead!" Lisa has given me permission to relate her story in some detail.

Katy and I saw her struggle, so we approached her about whether she would be willing to look closer at this issue with the Lord. Lisa indicated that she was disturbed by the voices that she heard in her head that hated men and that she was ready to be free of them. She agreed to meet with us to receive healing in this area.

Lisa came from a very dysfunctional family. Her mother had been raped by three men when she was in college, and this trauma had created huge issues in her life. Lisa's father was an alcoholic who was not responsible for his family, didn't generate enough income, and had very little relationship with his daughters. We knew that these factors had certainly contributed to Lisa's present difficulties with men.

During our first session with Lisa we identified that she had a judgment on men buried deep within her heart. During the second session, we began working through this judgment. We all agreed that finding the source of the lie that "men are bad" and discovering where that judgment began was where we needed to start.

We began by asking the Lord to reveal the point at which Lisa had embraced the lie as well as revealing the source and origin of the lie. The Lord very quickly showed Lisa a picture of a heart with a lock on it.

We prayed again, asking for further revelation, and the Lord took Lisa back one memory at a time until she was five years old. More than anything these memories revealed that Lisa was carrying extreme amounts of fear, which would have to be dealt with at some point. The memories also carried with them a theme that "men will not take care of you." As Lisa progressed through the memories we agreed that we were all getting the sense that this judgment on men had begun in the womb. It seemed that this judgment had been transferred to Lisa at birth and was reinforced all throughout her life in a million ways. The lie was already present in every memory the Lord brought to the surface. From as far back as she could remember, Lisa had embraced the lie that "men are bad."

After establishing that the lie had been a part of her life since birth, I told Lisa that I wanted to go back to the heart with the lock on it. I asked her if she would be willing to give Jesus the key to that lock. This approach presented a problem for Lisa because if she let Jesus unlock that bolt, the door of her heart would fly open and she would be open and exposed to men. She became very fearful. She also reported that she had seen a large root, like a bulb of a plant, with big roots growing out of it as we were praying. Katy then asked her if she would be willing to let Jesus cut down that root. That sounded less threatening to Lisa. She said that she was willing to let Jesus open the lock on her heart or dig out the root, so we went to the Lord in prayer and asked Him to do what He wanted.

Lisa soon reported that Jesus had returned to the picture. She was aware that she had gone back behind the door of her heart and shut the door. She knew immediately that she had to confess this sin and lack of trust. She voiced this confession and immediately reported that Jesus had reached out and opened the door. She was overwhelmed by the fact that the door wasn't locked, it wasn't even latched! She was not a prisoner behind that closed door; she was choosing to be in there. She then reported that the Lord had picked her up and carried her out of the room.

After Lisa had been freed from the bondage that had held her for so long, we then turned our attention to the room itself. Katy didn't want to leave the room accessible so that Lisa could run into it again if the going got tough. Lisa agreed that something needed to be done about that room. We prayed again and asked Jesus what He wanted to do about it. Lisa related that after we prayed Jesus put her down, took her by the hand, and walked with her to the edge of her heart. As they looked into her heart, Lisa saw a garden of huge weeds (representing all the lies about men that had kept her imprisoned). He showed her that underneath this garden of lies was a huge root. This huge root represented the judgment against men. Lisa asked the Lord what they were going to do about the root. He told her that she was going to have to trust Him. At that point, Lisa began to stall and couldn't respond.

Fear had gripped her powerfully at the thought of what the Lord might do. She told us about her difficulty and we prayed with her to release her from fear. She was then able to move forward with the Lord. She reported that the Lord grabbed the huge root and pulled on it, pulling everything else with it as well. He then tossed it aside. Then He showed her a beautiful garden of little plants that represented the million truths that Lisa had been taught over the years. He was watering them, and Lisa and the Lord were smiling at each other.

At this point we felt it was time to move into deliverance. We challenged any demonic attachments to this judgment. As we prayed Lisa complained of numb hands and a dizzy head. She could see the strong "men hating" spirit running around in her head that was always shouting, "I hate men!" Suddenly, instead of saying, "I hate men!" he started to scream, "I hate you!" At this point Lisa stopped the deliverance for a few minutes and reported more deeply on what she was experiencing. It was an incredible revelation to her that the spirit that was causing her to hate her husband, really hated her! She wept at the thought. After processing this new revelation for a few moments we returned to deliverance. As we prayed Lisa renounced this spirit and reported that she saw the Lord throw him into the abyss. After that she could see smaller, black spirits going out of her head and leaving her body. She was amazed!

As we closed in prayer, the Lord continued to speak to Lisa. He revealed to her that He would replace the root of judgment and bitterness in her heart with the truths of His Word, and that He would water them and help her to walk in them.

The next week, Lisa told us about how the Lord had worked between our counseling sessions. She told us that He had impressed upon her mind the word "life" and showed her that there was no life in that root anymore since it had been pulled out. As the vision continued throughout the day following our appointment, the root kept getting longer and longer. She was keenly aware of how long and deep the root of judgment against men ran in her heart. That root was pulled out and no longer had any life. She saw that there was no life in the judgment on men; it didn't protect her – in fact, that judgment actually bred death. She rejoiced in this truth and in the fact that the demon that hated her had been evicted!

This was only the beginning of God's new work in Lisa's life. In session after session we watched as He gently led her in the path of healing and deliverance. Nevertheless, the destruction of the root of judgment against men was a major turning point in her life. I asked Lisa to tell me what changes she had seen in her life since the Lord had worked in this area. The effects follow in her own words:

> It is now July of the same year [our ministry together was in the spring] and since that time I have experienced amazing freedom in this area. The first observation that I made after the judgment was gone was that I was actually able to "hear" men when they spoke. I was sitting in the living room of a friend and I realized that I was hearing him for the first time. I could hear every word he said. There were no voices to interfere. It was awesome! I could hear his words, but more than that, I could understand what he was saying which gave me the ability to know him on a deeper level. This wonderful freedom to hear and know men without judgment expanded to other men in my life.
>
> The second big change for me was the lack of fear when working with men in authority over me. I would always become fearful when someone in authority over me wanted to talk to me about something. The result of that fear was a judgment on them. I would make judgments on them in my heart and secretly hate them. This vanished after my deliverance. What freedom!!!
>
> Thirdly, I am able to interact with my husband on a completely different level. There are no voices screaming in

my head. No static. I am able to stay calm and work through conflict with him while staying in close proximity to him. My reflected sense of self seems to have vanished and I can maintain who I am when he is upset without judging him. It is wonderful.

It has been a great blessing to see the changes in Lisa's life. When she came to us she testified that her judgments on men were so deep that if she walked through a public place she would judge every man that passed her. In her mind she would decide that this one was an alcoholic, that one was cheating on his wife, that one was abusing his children, and so on. She was unable to see the truth about men and relate to them in healthy ways. The Lord has made a radical change in her life.

Praise God for His wonderful work in Lisa's life, and in the lives of many other brothers and sisters in Christ who have found freedom from ungodly judgments. May many more believers walk in this freedom and, by applying the teachings of Scripture, learn what it means to let God be judge.

CONCLUSION

Over the past few years our ministry team has been granted the opportunity to engage in prayer counseling with hundreds of believers in the country of Indonesia. We have been privileged to help them find freedom from rejection, bitterness, marital problems, sexual issues, relational difficulties, bondage to the occult, and a host of other personal problems and struggles. In the course of our ministry, we have observed that a major root of many problems is the ungodly judgments people make. When we lead them in forgiving those who have wronged them, in repenting of the judgments they have made, and in breaking their power, wonderful things happen in their lives and relationships. The results can be truly miraculous! Believers who were struggling and unable to grow in the Lord are brought into a new freedom and joy in Christ.

Judgments and the health of the Church

As we consider the importance of resolving ungodly judgments in the life of the Church of Jesus Christ, two areas of concern come to mind: the health of the Church and the mission of the Church. As the reader may have gathered from the discussion in the preceding chapters, this teaching and ministry is critical to the growth and sanctification of individual believers. We have already explored the sobering consequences of judging others, both in our lives and in the lives of others. The simple fact is that many believers are hindered in their walk with the Lord and in their relationships with others by the judgments they have made. They faithfully attend worship services, begin each day with Scripture reading and prayer, and gather together with other Christians in small group Bible studies, yet their relationship with God and their growth in Christ are hindered by the judgments that are buried deep within their hearts and minds. Only the Holy Spirit can root out these judgments and set them free to grow in Christ and to bear fruit for His glory. Therefore, careful and systematic teaching is critical so that believers can recognize their need, repent of their judgments against God, themselves, and others, and open their hearts to the healing work of the Holy Spirit.

Dealing effectively with ungodly judgments is critical not only to the spiritual health of individual believers, but also to the health of local churches. Why is this? For one thing, churches can only be healthy and strong when their individual members are healthy and growing in Christ, i.e. when they are free from the influence of ungodly judgments. Also, since healthy relationships between pastors, other church leaders, and members of a congregation can only develop in the absence of ungodly judgments, clear and systematic teaching on judgments is critical to the development of Christian fellowship that brings glory to God and that stimulates the growth of individual believers. Without this teaching, judgments inevitably occur. And where ungodly judgments are present, individual believers are separated by invisible walls, namely negative assumptions, expectations, and interpretations.

Judgments and the outreach of the Church

Clear and systematic teaching on resolving ungodly judgments is also critical so that the Church can make a strong testimony and lead many people to a saving knowledge of Jesus Christ. The fact is that nothing turns non-Christians off like a judgmental spirit. That is just the way it is. That does not mean, of course, that we should not stand for right and wrong, but it does mean that we need to speak the truth in a loving and gracious way. The fact is, however, that Christians often fail in this respect. Non-Christian family, friends, and co-workers are often appalled to see the way believers judge each other. And if that is not bad enough, we often judge them because they do not share our beliefs or do not live up to our behavioral norms. This type of judgment is absurd if you think of it, because they do not yet know Christ or live in the power of the Holy Spirit. They cannot be expected to live like Christians when they have yet to receive Christ as Savior and Lord. And yet we often judge them based on a standard that they are unable to keep. In the end, our judgmental spirit only drives them away from the Lord and His grace. For these reasons, repenting of ungodly judgments and breaking their power is essential if the Church is going to have a strong testimony in the coming days before Christ returns in glory. We can only be truly effective in reaching out and making disciples if we learn to practice a lifestyle of letting God be judge.

CPSIA information can be obtained
at www.ICGtesting.com
Printed in the USA
BVHW092141171118
533367BV00002B/296/P